D1209427

Starting With Assessment

A Developmental Approach to Deaf Children's Literacy

By Martha M. French

Pre-College National Mission Programs

Gallaudet University, Washington, D.C.

Copyright © 1999 by Pre-College National Mission Programs
Gallaudet University, Washington, D.C.
Library of Congress Card Catalog Number: 99-72137
ISBN Number 0-88095-221-0

ALL RIGHTS RESERVED. This book and parts thereof may not be reproduced in any form or by any means, electronic or mechanical, including photocopy, recording, or any information storage and retrieval system now known or to be invented, without written permission from the publisher, except in cases of brief quotations embodied in scholarly articles or reviews.

Note: THE ACCOMPANYING TOOLKIT SECTION **MAY** BE PHOTOCOPIED.

Cover and interior design by Shawn Neal Mahshie.
Photos by Judith Goodman and Frank Van Riper, as well as various PCNMP teachers and staff.

Permission to reprint the framework for literacy assessment from *Evaluating Literacy: A Perspective for Change* (Anthony, R. J.,;Johnson, T. D.; Mickelson, N. I.,; & Preece, A.; 1991; p.31) is granted from Heinemann Educational Books, Inc., Portsmouth, New Hampshire.

Permission to describe and quote from *The Primary Language Record Handbook* (Barrs, M.; Ellis, L.; Hester, H.; Thomas, A.; 1988, Heinemann Educational Books, Inc., Portsmouth, New Hampshire) is granted by the authors.

To receive additional copies of this document, or a complete listing of other Clerc Center publications, please contact:

Laurent Clerc National Deaf Education Center
Product Inquiries
KDES PAS-6
800 Florida Avenue, NE
Washington, DC 20002-3695
1-800-526-9105 (TTY/V), 202-651-5340 (TTY/V),
or 202-651-5708 (FAX)
E-mail: products.clerccenter@gallaudet.edu

Gallaudet University's Laurent Clerc National Deaf Education Center (formerly Pre-College National Mission Programs) is pleased to disseminate the information contained in this publication. The activities reported in this publication were supported by federal funding. Publication of these activities shall not imply approval or acceptance by the U.S. Department of Education of the findings, conclusions, or recommendations herein.

Gallaudet University is an equal opportunity employer/educational institution and does not discriminate on the basis of race, color, sex, national origin, religion, age, hearing status, disability, covered veteran status, marital status, personal appearance, sexual orientation, family responsibilities, matriculation, political affiliation, source of income, place of business or residence, childbirth, or any other unlawful basis.

Contents

Chapter 1 — 1

Chapter 2 — 23

Chapter 5   *123*

Chapter 6   *149*

References   *179*

Index   *187*

This Book

What it's About...

This book, including the separately bound appendices in *The Toolkit,* is about assessing the literacy development of children who are deaf. The book examines assessment philosophies and tools that can guide educational planning during the preschool and elementary years. It describes a model of assessment for written language—reading and writing—that covers multiple areas of learning and stresses the importance of conversational language to literacy development. An important premise of the model is that assessment should guide instruction according to the developmental needs of individual children.

The main ideas of the chapters are that *literacy assessment should:*

> ▶ build from principles that are grounded in current theories of learning (**Chapter 1**),

> ▶ define individual development—strengths and needs—according to multiple areas of learning and recognized stages of development (**Chapter 2**),

> ▶ describe (rather than measure with numbers) learning for young children with a variety of procedures (**Chapter 3**),

> ▶ involve others—the children, parents, colleagues—in the assessment process (**Chapter 4**),

> ▶ maintain records that will reflect a child's development over time and from different perspectives (**Chapter 5**), and

> ▶ complement and support an instructional program based on the same theories of learning suggested to support assessment (**Chapter 6**).

Who it's for...

This book, and the accompanying *Toolkit*, are for educational communities serving children who are deaf or hard of hearing. The information includes theoretical discussion, practical suggestions, and information about assessment for educators at all levels. The scope is broad for two reasons:

1) *Understanding why* practices are suggested, especially if they imply change, is a prerequisite to making more effective, flexible decisions about their use in the classroom. Educators need to consider the practical suggestions in this book in the context of changing theories in the areas of assessment, literacy instruction, and the education of deaf children.

2) *Consistency* is critical to program effectiveness. Everyone in a program must be "on the same page" to make changes that will be effective for students over the course of their development. Hence the ideal audience for this book is not just individual teachers, but the entire school community. What's more, everyone in this community must work together to build an effective program.

How One Might Use it...

Considering the emphasis on program consistency, this book and the *Toolkit* are most effectively used as a study guide within a school program or teacher preparation setting. However, whether working through the material independently or as a group, consider the following process:

▶ Read to understand the main ideas of each chapter—each chapter presents an important feature of a program for literacy assessment.

▶ Compare your own assessment program to the premise in each chapter. Decide which features are already in place and how effective they are. Decide, too, which are not in place or which need to be changed.

▶ Develop reasonable plans for making change. Include a timeline.

▶ Use the book and the *Toolkit* along with other referenced sources of information about classroom assessment as resources for implementing new procedures and techniques.

How it's Arranged...

The relationship between the book chapters and the *Toolkit* is illustrated in the chart below. Basically, the book lays out the important features of a classroom assessment program for literacy, the main ideas listed earlier. The *Toolkit* includes examples of assessment procedures and additional information about instructional activities that complement the assessment principles. The appendices are ordered in the *Toolkit* as they are introduced in the chapters.

Chapters	Related Appendices in *The Toolkit*
Chapter One *Starting With Assessment*	
Chapter Two *Building a Developmental Picture of Literacy*	**Appendix A, A-1** • Stages of Literacy Development • Literacy Profiles
Chapter Three *Assessment in the Classroom: Monitoring Learning, Informing Instruction*	**Appendix B, B-1, C, D, E** • Kendall Conversational Proficiency Levels Supplement to the P-Levels • Reading Checklists (Early Reading and Reading) • Kendall School Writing Levels • Guidelines for determining reading grade level
Chapter Four *Assessment as a Collaborative Effort: Involving Others in the Process*	**Appendix F** • Student and Parent Surveys
Chapter Five *Record Keeping*	(refers to **Appendices A-E**)
Chapter Six *Planning for Literacy Instruction*	**Appendix G** • Activities for a Balanced Reading and Writing Program at Different Levels of Development

About the Author

Martha Manson French, M.Ed., is an educational writer in reading development with the Success for All Foundation, Inc.—a comprehensive program for restructuring elementary schools. For many years she was employed with Pre-College National Mission Programs at Gallaudet University, where she worked to develop and facilitate the implementation of the language arts program for Kendall Demonstration Elementary School. Prior to that, Ms. French worked in programs for deaf children in a variety of capacities: as a teacher-trainer for language arts, as a teacher-resource specialist, as an elementary school teacher, and as a dormitory counselor for high school students. She has been a frequent contributor in the past to *Perspectives in Education and Deafness* and other publications with articles about language and literacy, and has presented workshops on literacy instruction and assessment to numerous groups of educators. She also co-authored with Joy Kreeft Peyton the Pre-College publication, *Making English Accessible: Using Electronic Networks for Interaction in the Classroom.*

Author's Note: Terminology

While the principles discussed in this book apply to all children, the specific discussions are meant to apply to those deaf and hard of hearing children who rely primarily on visual information in their social and academic environment.

Throughout this book, then, the single term, *deaf*, is used to refer to deaf or hard of hearing children who learn and communicate visually—children who, from birth or early childhood, do not have *full access* to **auditory** information. There are many variables surrounding how a deaf or hard of hearing person chooses to label him- or herself. Therefore, it is important to note that the general distinction made by the author is not about degree of hearing loss or cultural orientation, but whether or not a child tends to rely primarily on auditory or visual information as a primary receptive channel of communication—a distinction that has an important impact on how literacy assessment and instruction are approached.

The assessment tools presented in the appendices may be useful for assessing aspects of many older deaf students' literacy development, and the broad concepts addressed in this book are applicable to all students. However, the tools and discussions were primarily aimed at those in early childhood and elementary programs. Hence the term *children* (rather than *students*) will be used throughout this text.

Background and Acknowledgements

This book has its roots in discussions about reading assessment that began during the 1993-94 school year at the Kendall Demonstration Elementary School, part of Pre-College National Mission Programs (PCNMP), Gallaudet University. I want to begin by thanking fellow members of the Reading Assessment Group: Angela Bednarczyk, Margaret Hallau, William Kachman, Don Mahoney, Marsha Morales, and Rita Laporta. Lenard Kelly, of the Gallaudet Research Institute, was also a member of that group and contributed substantially to our understanding of reading.

I want to extend special thanks to Margaret Hallau, presently director of Exemplary Programs and Research, PCNMP. As former director of Curriculum Development, Research, and Evaluation for Pre-College, she guided my work in assessment for a number of years. Thanks, Margaret, for your excellent supervision and support.

The discussions in that Reading Assessment Group led to the development of a model for assessing reading. More than seventy copies of the model were sent to educators across the United States and in other countries who responded to an invitation in *Perspectives* to review the information (see *Perspectives*, 14, (3): So you want to assess student reading? Have we got a deal for you!). I am indebted to the individuals who took the time and effort to respond with their insights and wisdom. Their responses made the work a collaborative project that extended well beyond Kendall Demonstration Elementary School (KDES) to reflect the diversity that exists in programs and efforts aimed at educating deaf children.

I'm especially grateful to the teachers at KDES who reviewed the model, or parts of the model for assessing reading. Among these are: Lettie Bogatz, Judy Giannotti, Judy Phau, Margaret Simpson, Sharon Sandoval, Nancy Topolosky, and Janet Weinstock. These teachers gave feedback, tried checklists and forms, and, in some cases, let me come into their classrooms to try procedures myself.

From the beginning, we planned for the model of reading assessment to become a model for literacy assessment. Gradually the pieces came together, primarily in response to requests for information from various programs about instruction and assessment in reading and writing. In particular, development was furthered through preparation for the reading and writing workshops for representatives from the North Carolina State Schools for the Deaf in1996-1997. I am grateful to the North Carolina schools for the opportunity these workshops afforded me.

The model for literacy assessment would never have been articulated as it is here, however, if it were not for Shawn Mahshie. Shawn suggested that I propose publication of the materials and ideas for literacy assessment to the Pre-College National Mission Programs. I'm forever grateful to you, Shawn, for paving the way for this publication and to others at PCNMP, particularly the vice president, Jane Fernandes, for allowing it to happen. The opportunity has enabled me to record in full and share my thoughts about the influence literacy assessment should have on the instruction of deaf children.

I cannot claim full credit for these ideas, however. Some of the tools presented here were developed by others for KDES (e.g., the Kendall Conversational Proficiency Levels and the Kendall School Writing Levels). I've also learned much from deaf colleagues and children with whom I've worked. Along with the knowledge I've gained from these individuals, I've learned, too, my limitations as a hearing person to respond to any issue concerning literacy for people who are deaf. In that respect, I'm most humble in presenting the information here to the Deaf community. I'm well aware of its boundaries.

As I worked on this book, various individuals read sections and gave me feedback. I rely heavily on this part of the writing process and owe a great deal to anyone who was willing to be involved. Those who reviewed parts included: Angela Bednarczyk, Margaret Hallau, Judy Lenard, Jane Nickerson, Dave Schelper, Lenard Kelly, and Judy Mounty, from (or formerly with) Gallaudet University; Mary Martone, of the New Mexico School for the Deaf; Pam Shaw at the Kansas School for the Deaf, Marcia Volpe at the Pennsylvania School for the Deaf in Philadelphia; Peter V. Paul at The Ohio State University; Nancy Taylor at The Catholic University of America; Leslie Ridgeway, Melissa Rosenberg, and Trisha Schmirler, friends whose judgement and honesty I trust.

A few of these individuals deserve special mention. Peter V. Paul was kind enough to give me feedback on a substantial part of this material and greatly influenced me with his book, *Literacy and Deafness* (1998, Allyn and Bacon). Jane Nickerson deepened my understanding of portfolio use with deaf students by sharing her dissertation on work in that area (thanks, too, Jane, for letting me use your *Handbooks in Reading Research*). Judy Lenard—friend, neighbor, and former co-worker—deserves credit for passing work back and forth between Shawn at Gallaudet and me at home for almost two years without complaining!

I also want to thank members of the Office of Publications and Marketing at PCNMP who worked with me on this book: Randall Gentry, director; Shawn Mahshie, managing editor; Catherine Valcourt, production editor, for proofreading; and Mary Ellen Carew for copy editing support. I include Ken Kurlychek in this group, too, for his technical support with divider page photos and in production of the cover graphics. These individuals contributed publication expertise to the project that exemplified a high level of professionalism. Shawn, however, goes beyond that. Steeped as she is in the bilingual instruction of deaf children, she contributes knowledge of the subject of literacy development in addition to her excellent editing and formatting skills.

Finally, I want to thank my family for giving me room to do this project at home. It often spilled over into their time and space. They tolerated me frequently monopolizing the computer, often working during what should have been family time, always leaving papers spread around, and many times putting the project before them. Without my husband's patience and support, we couldn't have done it. And so I dedicate this book to them—my husband, Hugh French, and my sons, Adam and Taylor.

Starting With Assessment

Chapter 1

Principles of Literacy Assessment

Theories of Learning

Criticisms of Traditional Assessment

Modifying Procedures Based on Theories of Learning

Developmental Assessment

Conclusion

Starting With Assessment

I am an ardent believer in designing instruction for children based on need. But how do we know what the need is unless we have a means for gathering...data and analyzing it? So my picture of good teaching always starts with assessment and evaluation....

(R. C. Owen, electronic discussion, March, 1997)

*Assessment refers to "...the global process of synthesizing information about individuals in order to **understand and describe them** better."*

(Brown, as cited in McTighe & Ferrara, 1994; emphasis added)

This book is about assessing deaf children's literacy development in the classroom. The quotes above were selected because they support two important premises about the topic: that assessment should guide instruction and that, in order to do so, it must be descriptive. Stated simply, good literacy teaching should start by describing what children can and cannot do.

Assessment and instruction should be cyclical; each process should inform the other. Therefore, assessment should utilize the best available information about deaf children and literacy learning. While there are unresolved pieces in the puzzle of deaf children's literacy learning (there are for hearing children as well), much is now known that has yet to be applied.

Incorporating state-of-the-art theory and findings from research into existing instructional practices is the essence of school reform—an effort that deaf[1] children deserve.

Reform, however, implies change and should be approached systematically to be effective. The process starts when the individuals that make up a school community work together to define principles that will guide new practices, then make a commitment to them. Positive differences in student achievement will depend on how successfully the details of these principles are thought through, implemented, and adjusted with actual practice—not just by individuals, but by educational programs as a whole. Programs for deaf children that succeed in implementing more current principles for literacy assessment will systematically do the following:

▶ Involve parents and children in assessment.

▶ Emphasize early language acquisition and experiential learning.

▶ Capitalize on motivation, student collaboration, and reflective thinking in the learning process.

▶ Demonstrate that concepts about first and second language learning are relevant for many children.

These and other important characteristics of literacy learning for deaf children should be reflected in assessment procedures and evident in record keeping. In short, they should *inform* instruction.

The Developmental Principle

For the reasons above, this book starts by proposing guiding principles for assessment—a mental checklist of sorts for individuals and for programs. One of these principles—that assessment should be developmental—represents an underlying theme throughout the book. It reinforces the importance of conversational language to learning to read and write. It nudges assessment to take a holistic view of the growth of literacy—a view that stresses the need for open-ended, descriptive observations of students. The developmental principle encourages teachers to view students' "errors" as sources of information about need, rather than weaknesses or mistakes. It also leads to assessment that will facilitate instruction guided by knowledge of students' strengths as well as their instructional needs.

---

[1] See Author's Note on Page "x" for discussion of this and other terms as used in this book.

This important principle points to using the sequential stages of development and the milestones of achievement associated with each stage to examine individual students' patterns of growth (e.g., Chall, 1983; Krashen, 1992; O'Donnell & Wood, 1992). It indicates that knowledge about students comes from two sources:

1. the broad developmental stages identified for groups of children, and
2. each child's individual pattern of development within that framework.

In that context, the assessment of literacy targets instruction according to what individual children *have learned* and what they *are ready to learn next*.

In summary, the developmental principle and other principles introduced lay important groundwork for subsequent chapters that examine a framework of planning for assessment. This framework, which rests on the principles discussed in this chapter, includes:

▶ locating students' competencies within broad, developmental levels;

▶ selecting methods that will support this goal and monitor progress individually;

▶ involving others in assessment, including students themselves and parents;

▶ organizing assessment with systematic, long-term record keeping; and

▶ building complementary and parallel practices for instruction.

Principles of Literacy Assessment

> *...the main legitimate purpose of evaluation in education is to guide instruction (p.187).*
>
> Zemelman et al. (1993)

The principles described here support both the general goal for classroom assessment and the specific goals for literacy assessment. According to Popham (1995), the purpose of all classroom assessment is to inform instruction by monitoring students' progress with respect to different variables.

Shanklin and Rhodes (1993) describe more specifically the aims of assessing literacy according to the International Reading Association's resolutions on this issue. They expand these aims, all of which relate to learning and instruction, to define what they see as seven purposes of assessment for literacy (p. 5):

"For the guidance and improvement of learning..."

- to determine what development is occurring
- to identify a student's strengths and weaknesses in reading and writing

"[For] the guidance and improvement of instruction..."

- to discover the power of your teaching
- to learn more about the development of reading and writing
- to sharpen the quality of your observations and your confidence in them

"[For] monitoring the outcomes of instruction..."

- to have information about a student as a reader and writer to share with others.
- to assess program strengths and weaknesses and guide staff

These goals have led to changes in assessment practices that have been gaining in popularity in recent years. The changes point to the principles listed and described below. Put into practice, these principles lead to assessment that is more consistent with what is known about the development of literacy.

The assessment of literacy should be:

- based on current theories
- developmental
- authentic
- comprehensive and balanced
- an ongoing part of instruction
- inclusive—involve students, parents, and others in the school
- supported by a well-developed system of record keeping
- designed to inform instruction

The assessment of literacy should be based on current theories (e.g., Anthony et al., 1991; Routman, 1991): We know more today about learning, the development of literacy, deaf children, and assessment. As mentioned earlier, educators should use this information to make changes in educational practices.

Assessment should be consistent with "the best scholarship on language, learning, teaching, and curriculum" (Goodman, 1989). However, theories should not be used to promote any one approach to either instruction or assessment over consideration of individual children. Instead, theories should be used flexibly to support practices according to individual need and development, as indicated in the next principle.

The assessment of literacy should be developmental (e.g., Rhodes & Shanklin, 1993): As previously discussed, assessment must come from a developmental, child-centered perspective in order to facilitate instruction. Summarizing the points of that discussion, this principle guides assessment to do the following.

> ▶ Examine students' strengths and needs, including information about error patterns, background knowledge, and interests.

> ▶ View literacy as the *interdependent* growth of language, reading, writing, and other related variables.

> ▶ Monitor growth over time, using knowledge about recognized stages of development to understand individual patterns.

Activities for assessing literacy should be authentic (e.g., Calfee & Hiebert, 1991; Rhodes & Shanklin, 1993): Assessment should be "authentic"—it should occur within natural, meaningful acts of conversational language use, reading, and writing. The rich context of such activities enables students to actively apply what they know to the task—their linguistic and experiential knowledge. When assessment is authentic, students are aware of the purpose of the activity and are therefore likely to have more motivation to perform. Further, authentic, "holistic," assessment avoids splintering tasks into isolated skills that may not reflect actual performance in literacy.

The assessment of literacy should be comprehensive and balanced (e.g., Anthony et al., 1991; Calfee & Hiebert, 1991; McTighe & Ferrara, 1994): Assessment should be both comprehensive and balanced in terms of *what* it evaluates and *how* it evaluates. This principle, labeled "multifaceted" by Routman (1991), suggests that assessment take into account process and product, information from observational as well as measurement procedures, data from multiple contexts, and information from multiple sources. This principle is central to capturing an ongoing picture of students' development under the influence of many variables, including culture and experience. It is the pooling of this data—the process of *triangulating* information from multiple methods and sources—that enables teachers to make valid decisions about their students' strengths and instructional needs.

The assessment of literacy should be an ongoing part of instruction (e.g., McTighe & Ferrara, 1994): "Centered in the classroom" is another way of describing this principle (Anthony et al., 1991). Yetta Goodman's suggestion that assessment should be a "seamless part of instruction" is in response to the criticism that traditional assessment has been "decontextualized." Although balanced assessment of literacy includes a variety of kinds of methods, traditional assessment does not provide the detailed data about student development that can be obtained with observational methods. Routman (1991) believes that teachers should emphasize informal, observational assessment in the classroom because it aligns more closely with instruction activities. Many teachers have devised convenient ways to record their observations without drawing time or attention away from instruction. An understanding of the processes of literacy and knowledge about development must inform observational assessment. This information indicates what to look for and how to interpret what one sees.

The assessment of literacy should involve students, parents, and others in the school community (e.g., Rhodes & Shanklin, 1993; Tierney et al., 1991): There are many facets to this principle, or ways students, parents, and others should be involved in assessment. First of all, those who know a student—and certainly the student him- or herself—have information that contributes to the teacher's picture of development. By structuring ways to obtain this kind of information, teachers add another dimension to what they know from their own assessments. They also build ways for students to reflect on their learning. In addition, students, parents, and support personnel come to feel that they are partners with the teacher in the educational process.

Conversely, students, parents, and support personnel benefit from what teachers have learned through their assessments. This kind of communication—teacher to others—should be routine and descriptive in nature. It can become a powerful tool for informing others about the development of literacy, as well as another way of involving these individuals in the assessment process. This kind of communication is also essential in helping students become more metacognitive. By receiving descriptive information about their progress from teachers, they become better at reflecting upon their strengths, needs, and strategy use, and participating in their own goal setting. Ultimately, this helps place the final responsibility for learning with the students, one of Routman's (1991) beliefs about assessment.

The assessment of literacy should include a system of record keeping (e.g., Routman, 1991; Tierney et al., 1991): Without a record keeping system, students, parents, teachers, and others involved in instruction cannot share assessment data successfully or use it to verify instructional decisions. Without systematic documentation, assessment cannot show longitudinal growth nor can it demonstrate patterns of development resulting from relationships among the major areas of literacy—conversational language, reading, and writing. Further, students cannot use it to monitor their own progress. Record keeping is a necessary part of assessment if it is to guide instruction in literacy. It should involve students as well as teachers, reflect the development of literacy as a whole (including all areas of development), describe strengths as well as needs, and examine progress over time (beyond the current year).

The assessment of literacy should inform instruction (e.g., Calfee & Hiebert, 1991; Paul, 1998; Rhodes & Shanklin, 1993; Routman, 1991; Tierney et al., 1991): This principle speaks to the heart of the main purpose for assessment—to guide instruction. It implies that assessment should:

- be descriptive rather than summative (measured),

- describe strengths as well as needs in keeping with the developmental principle,

- be noncompetitive (focused on the individual), and

- lead to decisions based on information from multiple sources and multiple contexts.

In a sense, the assessment of literacy is successful in directing instruction—informing teaching and learning—to the degree that it adheres to the other principles.

In keeping with the goal for assessment, the principles presented here are those that should be used to *guide instruction*. They are supported by discussions of principles in a number of texts about the assessment of literacy. For example, Rhodes and Shanklin (1993) devote part of the first chapter of their book, *Windows into Literacy: Assessing Learners K-8*, to an explanation of these principles. Routman (1991) discusses her beliefs and corresponding goals for assessing literacy in a chapter on evaluation in *Invitations: Changing as Teachers and Learners K-12*. In *Portfolio Assessment in the Reading-Writing Classroom*, Tierney, Carter, & Desai (1991) conclude their chapter on the theory of assessment with "goals for classroom assessment" and "features of a classroom-based assessment program." There are other discussions in *Literacy and Deafness: The Development of Reading, Writing, and Literate Thought* (Paul, 1998) and *Evaluating Literacy: A Perspective for Change* (Anthony, Johnson, Mickelson, & Preece, 1991). These resources contribute to the assumptions about assessment discussed above.

In addition to suggesting new procedures, these principles imply what practices of assessment one should seek to avoid, as illustrated below (French, 1999):

The Assessment of Literacy *Should*:	The Assessment of Literacy *Should Not:*
• be theory-based	• be based on programmed guides for instruction that do not reflect current understanding of the development and assessment of literacy
• be developmental	• test sequenced lists of skills, regardless of need, or evaluate reading and writing separately from conversational language
• be authentic	• test isolated skills in exercises that are meaningless and do not involve real-world use of conversational and written language
• be comprehensive and balanced	• be limited to one or two evaluation procedures at any given time (especially if they are commercially developed tests)
• be an ongoing part of instruction	• take a lot of time to prepare, select, or administer; occur only periodically; be separate from instructional activities
• involve students, parents, and others in the school community	• be conducted and used by the teacher alone, excluding the student, parents, and others involved in instruction
• include a system of record keeping	• be recorded primarily with formal test results and report cards
• inform instruction	• focus on grades or scores, setting up a competitive atmosphere in which students compare their progress to their peers, rather than examine their own development

However, one cannot significantly change assessment practices simply with the selection of new procedures. Instead, individuals *and* programs must understand, internalize, and use principles such as those above in consistent ways that will affect instruction. In order to do so, it may help to review some of the more important theories of learning that support these principles and have led to changes in assessment.

Theories of Learning

Recent theories of learning have contributed to shifts in education. The theories indicate new directions for curricula and assessment by redefining learning as a cognitive process. In *A Practical Guide to Alternative Assessment*, Herman, Aschbacher, & Winters (1992) describe theories that appear to have had the most impact. These theories define learning as follows:

- Learning is an active, reflective process (Wittrock, 1979).

- Learning occurs holistically and is influenced by motivation.

- Learning taps multiple intelligences (Gardner, 1982).

- Learning is social in nature.

The theories represent some of the major changes in thinking about instruction for all children—deaf and hearing. They, and their impact on the literacy education of deaf children, are described below. Applied to assessment, these theories have led to dissatisfaction with traditional methods of assessment and have prompted the development of new methods. Translated into beliefs about practice, they have become the basis for principles of instruction and assessment such as those discussed in the previous section.

Learning is an active, reflective process
Learners are not passive recipients of information, as once thought, but active processors of what they are learning. They construct meaning by linking new information to what they already know—their existing schema (Anderson & Pearson, 1984). Many variables shape learning, including background knowledge, skills, and interests. This leads to unique, personal interpretations of information. This process includes processing new information but also learning how to use it—how to organize, structure, and solve problems. Reflection and self-monitoring ("Does this make sense to me? Why? How do I know?") are parts of this process.

This theory reflects the belief that children do not simply learn conversational language by mimicking or copying others. They bring innate abilities to the task, even compensating for insufficient models by creating linguistic rules

(Pinker, 1994). Language evolves out of functional context, as children bring to bear a complex, instinctive ability to the task. It "emerges" under the right conditions, both in and out of the classroom.

In the same manner, educators have come to view reading and writing as active processes of learning literacy. As with their learning of conversational language, children bring a great deal of information to the tasks of reading and writing. They use their prior knowledge, linguistic and experiential, to construct meaning when reading and to communicate thoughts in writing. As a result, these tasks are highly personal. In order to teach these tasks, educators need to know the following: how well developed children's knowledge is, how accurate it is, and how well they can apply what they know. Misconceptions children have can impede learning just as much as the lack of knowledge can. Assessment should include examining students' processes (as well as their products) of reading and writing, their background knowledge, their thinking, and their ability to reflect on what they know—their metacognitive skills. Using this information to inform instruction and increasing students' awareness of such information facilitate learning.

This theory applies as much to deaf students as to hearing students. Deaf and hearing children acquire conversational signed or spoken language naturally when they can see or hear the language input adequately, use it interactively, and experience it from an early age (Meier, 1991). However, these conditions fail to exist for many young deaf children. Deaf children also interact with print in the same ways that hearing children do, actively processing print by using linguistic cueing systems (semantic, syntactic, and graphophonic information) and background knowledge (Ewoldt, 1981). Deaf students, however, may vary greatly—from hearing children and from one another—in the nature of the information they possess and their application of it. This is due, in part, to differences in the scope and kind of conversational language to which they have been exposed, their early childhood experiences with literacy, and the approach of their educational program. Assessment must determine what each individual brings to the task of processing print—the nature and application of his or her linguistic cueing systems and background knowledge.

Learning occurs holistically and is influenced by motivation

Learning advances globally, expanding on broad, interdependent fronts with unique patterns of growth within each front. Variations in motivation and interest influence the uniqueness of these patterns. Also, at any point in development, learning involves both higher and lower level skills and strategies. In other words, it does not happen by acquiring a string of skills—beginning with those at the "lower" level—that build until an individual is "ready" to perform a complex task, such as reading.

For this reason, when a sequence of skills guides instruction for all students, many do not receive instruction geared to their needs. They may already have the skill, or it may be presented at the wrong time for their development—at a time when they are not ready to learn it. Furthermore, when students learn skills this way, as building blocks for performing tasks, they typically do not learn the skills in the context of the task itself. Thus, the skills often do not transfer to performance as expected. Also, students lose sight of the purpose of learning and become less motivated. Learning is best approached holistically with whole-to-part activities that are highly motivating and keep students focused on the purpose of the tasks.

This theory leads to the understanding that acquiring literacy is a developmental process involving a number of related, interdependent variables; it does not follow a sequenced hierarchy of skills. However, broad stages of development or tendencies exist. Individual growth may follow—or deviate from—these stages, since many factors, including culture and experience, influence each child's process. Further, the rate of individual development varies. For these reasons, growth through these recognized broad stages is still a unique process. As a result, one cannot teach literacy effectively with a set of objectives, even though commercial programs of instruction perpetuate this notion.

Although it sounds simplistic, individuals learn conversational and written language primarily by communicating with others, by reading, and by writing, both in the classroom and in other contexts. Feedback—both incidental and planned—facilitates this process. In the classroom, reading and writing should be kept whole, and above all, meaningful. Teachers should take into account what each child already knows and can do—what he or she brings to the classroom—according to knowledge of developmental stages. Assessment of this information should occur within the context of authentic activities (conversation, reading, and writing used for real world purposes).

Traditionally, deaf (as well as hearing) children have been taught conversational language, reading, and writing according to objectives in commercial materials or curricula. With this approach, children have studied rules and skills (sometimes for years) through drill and practice exercises, while the actual tasks of reading and writing were held off until they were "ready." *These students have had far too little experience with authentic reading and writing*. Also, research has confirmed teachers' findings in the classroom: acquiring these readiness skills has not necessarily resulted in the ability to perform the desired tasks. Further, goals for instruction have been established according to age or grade without regard for individual development, and are not necessarily appropriate for the individual student at the time.

Deaf students, as with all students, learn best when they learn skills within the context of meaningful activities. For example, many highly literate deaf adults indicate that they learned to read not from the instruction in their classroom, but from their own habits of voracious reading. Deaf children need instructional goals targeted to their personal strengths and needs and based on a broad view of literacy. Further, they need activities that make the use of conversational language, reading, and writing meaningful and relevant—activities that are intrinsically motivating.

Learning taps multiple intelligences

Conventional, standardized tests reflect the concept that there are two primary intelligences: verbal (linguistic) and nonverbal (mathematic). This concept has filtered down to the curriculum with teachers emphasizing these skills, hoping to raise students' standardized test scores. What we now know, however, is that there are multiple intelligences, including visual-spatial, kinesthetic, musical, personal (intrapersonal and interpersonal), and naturalistic, in addition to linguistic and mathematical (Checkley, 1997; Gardner, 1983). Although everyone has all of these intelligences, individuals vary greatly in their configuration, typically possessing strengths in several areas.

The theory of multiple intelligences has important implications for the way we teach in all areas of development. It prompts us to analyze how each student learns best, acknowledging that there are variations in style. Teachers should use this information to present material in ways that will accommodate these variations as much as possible, even though matching each personal style in a single lesson is probably impossible (Brualdi, 1996). It is more reasonable to expect teachers to be aware of differences, help students recognize their strengths, and build in opportunities for students to individualize their approach to activities. For example, students responding to literature might choose to tailor their responses in various ways. They might choose to illustrate parts of the story (visual-spatial), write about the story in a journal or retell it (linguistic), create a song about the story (musical), or dramatize the story with dance (kinesthetic). Procedures of assessment need to accommodate these variations in intellectual strengths and preferences, in addition to uncovering what they are.

In some cases, the emphasis on standardized testing of skills in the English language has penalized deaf children, especially those who are young. This is also true of the extensive use of achievement tests that rely on proficiency in written English. Many deaf students, whose first language is signed, are likely to develop these skills on a maturational schedule that is more closely associated with learning a second language. This makes written standardized tests, when given according to age or grade, unfair. These tests capitalize on linguistic intelligence and assume certain levels of development in that language. Further, they do so based on a language—English—that may not be the primary language for many children, deaf or hearing. The damage is even greater if such scores are emphasized over other types of assessment.

These practices have contributed to a deficit model of instruction, misconstruing students' "slower" development of written English as, at best, a major "weakness," and, at worst, a lack of intelligence. They deny many deaf students the opportunity to demonstrate linguistic intelligence in their primary language, American Sign Language (ASL), or to demonstrate their intelligences and knowledge in other areas through ASL. When teachers rely heavily on standardized test scores, the narrow perception of intelligence as either linguistic, measured according to skill in the English language, or mathematics may damage the students' self-esteem and limit their potential.

Instruction in deaf education needs to elevate recognition of multiple intelligences and push for assessment that reflects multiple abilities. Educators should also take into account the fact that members of Deaf culture, similar to those of other cultures, will value certain intelligences over others. Deaf people, too, are likely to perform better with tests that utilize their primary language, if it is not English. Using this information to facilitate instruction will likely increase students' self-esteem and the development of individual potential. Assessment that seeks to gather information about individual strengths will be open-ended and multifaceted.

Learning is social in nature

Instruction has traditionally focused on students working in isolation in classrooms that minimized discussion, noise, and distractions. The teacher's lecture has been the prevailing format for sharing information. Advances in the theory of learning, however, have uncovered the importance of the social nature of learning, setting into motion more collaborative, interactive classrooms. We now recognize that social interaction facilitates learning (Vygotsky, 1978). When students work together, they learn strategies and skills from each other and how to solve problems in a team. This powerful collaboration is often more effective than working alone in solving problems that require a higher order of thinking skills. It is certainly more typical of "authentic" problem solving in real life.

Literacy develops out of a need to communicate with others, both face-to-face and through print. We know that students best acquire skills in literacy within the context of whole, authentic activities (Pearson & Fielding, 1991). Social interaction is a natural consequence of these activities and is critical to "scaffolding" the development of literacy (Vygotsky, 1978). Scaffolding

(Bruner, 1975) occurs when interactions between a novice language user and a more experienced language user inform and gradually build up the skills of the novice. Feedback and modeling in language are examples of techniques inherent in such interactions. During reading and writing activities, scaffolding occurs as more experienced users of written language demonstrate their knowledge, skills, and strategies in these tasks. These more experienced students also serve as an audience for others and provide feedback. Encouraging interaction among students and between student and teacher enhances instruction in the classroom. These interactions are important opportunities for assessment, too, as they reveal information about students' knowledge, thought processes, and collaborative abilities.

The social nature of learning suggests that certain conditions must be in place in order for deaf students to experience interactive learning. First, the conversational language used in the classroom must be accessible to all students. If signed language is used, it should be fully accessible—comprehensible—to all students at all times. The same should be true if spoken language is used. In other words, spoken language should only be considered for academic purposes if a student can make full use of spoken language socially as well. Although these conditions for spoken language don't exist for many deaf students, the social use of English has become more accessible to many students in recent years through the use of computers. Electronic mail, Internet "chat" rooms, and computer networks used for instruction, such as Electronic Networks for Interaction (ENFI), have enabled students to interact in English with full accessibility (Peyton & French, 1996). Research has documented examples of language scaffolding in English that occur during these computer-mediated classroom conversations when more expert users of English converse with less proficient users (Peyton et al., 1993, p. 88).

For most deaf children, social interactions for learning depend upon the availability and use of a face-to-face, visual language. [According to Pettito (1993), a visual language is one of the "natural signed languages," such as ASL.] In order to use a visual language for social and instructional purposes in the classroom, however, the same conditions described above must apply—full accessibility to the language for all students at all times. Also, it is important to emphasize the following:

▶ The teacher must be able to use the language; he or she must also be proficient in the language in order to capitalize on students' interactions for assessment purposes.

▶ "Experts," or more proficient users of the signed language (other than the teacher) must be part of the class—those who can scaffold other students who are in the process of acquiring the language.

▶ It must be acknowledged by all that sign language will be used for instructional, as well as social, communications.

In summary, the theories described above suggest that assessment must change to better capture the learning process for individuals. Further, it is the inability of traditional assessment to meet this goal—to capture the best picture possible of the learning process for individual students—that has led to dissatisfaction with conventional practices to carry out the primary purpose of assessment. The next section will look at some of these shortcomings.

Criticisms of Traditional Assessment

One might describe traditional, or conventional, assessment as our educational system's emphasis on **summative** evaluation—the kind of evaluation that *quantifies* what has been learned so far with a numerical score. This contrasts with **formative** evaluation, which *describes* students' growth as well as their needs (e.g., Zemelman et al., 1993).

Criticisms of traditional measurement approaches to assessment are relatively new. The summative approach described above historically has satisfied many, if not most, of the purposes of assessment. For example, teachers have used grades and scores to evaluate students and communicate progress to them and their parents. Scores and grades have also been used to evaluate program effectiveness and to group students according to their abilities. Granted, some well-constructed tests have provided diagnostic information about errors in addition to measures of learning. However, critics say this approach to assessment, or our *reliance* on measurement, is inadequate, and even inappropriate, to use for many of these purposes. One complaint has been that the predominant use of standardized tests for grouping and placement purposes unfairly puts certain students in program "tracks" that limit their potential.

The primary criticism of conventional practices, especially the use of standardized tests, however, seems to be that they are inadequate for carrying out the main purpose of assessment: to guide instruction. Some of the reasons for this follow.

- The format of conventional tests typically includes multiple choice or true-false items. These items prompt students to select answers, rather than generate their own, and possibly miss information about what the students have learned.

- Conventional test items for reading typically include short passages of text written with carefully controlled vocabulary and syntax; such items limit the contextual support that longer passages of "real" literature provide.

- Conventional testing practices administer the same test to all students. It is possible, with this approach, to miss individual ways that students have of demonstrating what they know. Same-test administration to all students may also measure developmentally inappropriate objectives for some students.

- Traditional testing tends to separate assessment from instruction and, especially with standardized tests, may not accurately reflect what is being taught. Further, traditional testing often becomes another task teachers must prepare for and administer, siphoning time and energy away from instruction.

- Many traditional tests fail to measure higher-level thought processes or the application of knowledge. They are based on a linear, rather than holistic, concept of learning, as described earlier.

In summary, traditional assessment provides little constructive feedback to students about their performance and not enough information for teachers about instructional direction. Such criticisms are prompting educators to look for new methods that will more effectively fulfill the purpose of assessment. They are looking for methods and procedures that support current theories of learning.

Modifying Procedures Based on Theories of Learning

The learning theories described earlier that are behind criticisms of traditional assessment also point the way to new procedures in response to this call for change. Examples of these procedures include:

▶ checklists that facilitate observation by reflecting information about specific areas of development or tasks;

▶ portfolios that document the process of students' development in literacy, involving them in reflection of that process and personal goal setting;

▶ methods used to examine students' use of strategies (miscue analysis, running records, think-alouds);

▶ holistic scoring methods for analyzing writing samples; and

▶ procedures for recording "open-ended" observational information.

These new procedures are often referred to collectively as alternative assessment (e.g., Herman, et al., 1992). For example, assessments that examine students as they read and write, observing their use of strategies, and encouraging them to reflect on these strategies, demonstrate the active, reflective nature of learning. Such assessments examine metacognitive abilities and involve students in their own evaluations. The use of portfolios, which includes students in goal-setting and periodic review of their progress, is one way that teachers are examining process and including students in evaluation.

The holistic theory of learning, emphasizing whole-to-part instruction, has moved assessment away from monitoring progress strictly according to commercial curricula that teach—and assess—skills in a lock-step progression. This concept has brought to the forefront the idea of "kid-watching" (Goodman, 1986)—gathering and documenting observational kinds of data about students' performance. It posits that observing what students do during ongoing instructional activities provides a more complete picture of the students' skills than testing alone. Further, the whole-to-part theory of learning promotes assessment in the context of authentic tasks—the use of reading and writing in relation to purposeful communication—rather than assessment that tests individual skills out of context. In this way, both higher and lower level skills and strategies may be monitored.

The concept of multiple intelligences has led to more observational assessment practices. The use of tests alone—whether they are created by teachers or more formal, standardized tests—cannot capture the varied strengths and needs of individuals. Observation, in a variety of different contexts, helps teachers see not only what their students know, but also how they process and apply what they know. The need to view students in different contexts also indicates the importance of involving others in assessment—other professionals, parents, and the students themselves. The richness of this observational data becomes a window into students' strengths, especially as they demonstrate various intelligences and their use of strategies.

Recognition of the social nature of learning has led to more authentic assessments of performance in which students must work together to solve problems. These collaborative, performance-based tests more accurately replicate real-life problem solving situations and emphasize the value of group inquiry. By working together in groups, students learn effective thinking strategies from their peers; they also learn to give and accept constructive criticism and come to appreciate reaching goals through collaborative efforts.

A Developmental Approach to Assessment

Perhaps the most global impact that learning theories have had on assessment, however, is the movement to assess literacy developmentally, as pointed out in the beginning of this chapter. Taken collectively or examined separately, these theories indicate that literacy is a highly unique, developmental process. No two children come to the classroom with the same background knowledge, social experiences, or patterns of development and intelligences. Consequently, assessment needs to inform instruction by describing this process as fully and individually as possible and using that information to establish educational goals.

The concept of developmental here is different from the more traditional interpretation of the term. The traditional interpretation implies that students must learn to read and write competently before they can learn in other subject areas. It claims proficiency in reading and writing is a developmental prerequisite to learning in other subject areas.

This interpretation of the concept is manifest in the "developmental" classes for older students designed to improve their reading skills so they can learn in other disciplines (Bruce & Davidson, 1994). Applied to young children, this interpretation is evident in our elementary schools' focus on reading and the related language arts skills. However, the practices associated with this traditional concept of developmental—centering the curricula on reading and writing for a certain age-group—are being questioned, both for deaf and hearing children (e.g. Bruce & Davidson, 1994; Paul, 1998).

Used here, the term developmental refers to understanding the orderly progression of the development of literacy as background information for interpreting individual progress. Also, it defines literacy holistically—as a composite of multiple areas of development, not just reading and writing (text-based competencies). The perspective used throughout this book is that one should view these text-based competencies in the context of related areas in the development of literacy. Further, this view urges the reader to consider the development of literacy in the context of broader educational goals for deaf children—knowledge in all areas.

Conclusion

In summary, the principles of assessment described in this chapter are supported by theories of learning. Among these is the principle that assessment should be developmental. The use of these principles should result in practices that are descriptive and examine what children know as well as what they need to learn next.

The learning theories that support these principles are having an impact on assessment at all levels. For example, changes are occurring in many standardized tests. Notably, there are now standardized tests that include longer passages of natural text and items that elicit open-ended responses. These tests also analyze students' use of strategy in addition to their knowledge. Well-known examples of these, in the area of literacy, are the Illinois and Minnesota state-level tests. The Maryland School Performance Assessment Program is another example. This series of tests includes authentic problem-solving tasks that require students to work collaboratively. The most significant changes in assessment, however, have been occurring in the classroom as teachers redirect assessment to more effectively inform instruction.

The purpose of this chapter has been to lay the foundation for further discussions of assessing literacy in the classroom. Although the author acknowledges the need for traditional, measurement forms of assessment in a balanced program, the discussions in the remainder of this book will focus on the use of alternative means of assessing literacy for instructional purposes. In other words, the need for formal assessment—standardized testing—is recognized but not treated in this text. The reason for focusing on alternative, classroom assessment—aside from the fact that these methods are not as well known as traditional methods—is because of its potential to guide instruction. Alternative assessments can obtain a more accurate, complete picture of learning—one that can help develop more effective instruction for individuals.

The examples of assessment tools in the following chapters are just that—examples. They are presented to introduce new procedures but not necessarily to describe their use in detail. There is no assumption that the reader will adopt all of the tools or procedures provided here; it is likely that some may prove useful and others will not. These tools may lead to the selection of similar and perhaps more effective procedures, or they may reinforce those that are already being used. Teachers might use them, too, as examples for developing new procedures more tailored to their needs. Whatever the case, as long as the selection or creation of assessment tools and procedures supports the principles described in this chapter, teachers are likely to be accomplishing their goal—to improve instruction and learning.

Building a Developmental Picture of Literacy

Building a Developmental Picture of Literacy

Assessing individual strengths, needs, and broad patterns of development over time—within a view of literacy that examines multiple variables—should become the starting point for planning and instruction in literacy. This developmental perspective (Leslie, 1993; O'Donnell & Wood, 1992), the subject of this chapter, is based on the following concepts:

▶ The development of literacy involves the interdependent learning of conversational language, reading and writing, and related variables, including motivation and social interactions.

▶ There are recognized stages in the development of literacy—an order to the growth-related process of learning conversational language and written language, or reading and writing.

▶ Within each of these stages of development, there are major achievements in learning that are necessary to support advancement in subsequent stages.

▶ Instruction is most effective when it addresses (a) what a child needs to learn in order to progress within his or her present stage of development, and (b) unmet goals from previous stages, if any, that may ultimately hinder progress. The use of other curricular information and materials should support these goals, rather than determine the direction of instruction.

This chapter proposes that these concepts run counter to some common practices in literacy programs. Although the goal here is to suggest that changes in assessment and instruction might improve learning in this area, the reader is asked to view that goal within the context of a deaf student's—or any student's—broader educational goals. Learning to read and write should be part of a child's broader educational goals rather than stepping stones to these goals. Consider the following scenario:

A young child, recently diagnosed as deaf, is placed in an early childhood program. One of the main goals of the program is to facilitate the development of conversational language. Although the child makes progress, her or his language does not develop as quickly as a hearing child's. At the same age as hearing children, however, the deaf child enters an academic program where she or he is taught reading and writing with a curriculum that is organized by grade levels. "Literacy" is defined as competency in reading and writing, but those tasks are taught as separate subjects. Again, the child makes progress but quickly falls behind the progress expected in the curriculum for his or her grade. The greater the discrepancy between the child's performance in "literacy" (performance in reading and writing) and the curriculum expectations for his or her grade, the more concentrated the focus becomes on diagnosing and remediating the child's reading and writing skills.

In this scenario, *teaching* language—conversational and then written—is the goal of the child's educational program from preschool through the elementary years. Despite the best of intentions, however, programs frequently fail to achieve the language goals they so diligently pursue in literacy. This scenario typically ends in one of two ways:

1. The child continues to make progress learning to read and write but the gap between achievement and the goals for his or her grade, as determined with the curriculum, continues to widen. Everyone involved—teachers, parents, students—focuses on the fact that the child is making progress and pays less and less attention to the growing discrepancy between achievement and grade expectations.

2. *Or*, the child eventually plateaus and seems to be "stuck." Both the student and the teachers experience frustration, a sense of failure, and finally, apathy.

With either ending, there is an element of failure—failure in the sense that the child never learns according to his or her potential. Unfortunately, there are even those who come to view this as predictable—an unavoidable pattern in the education of deaf children. However, the scenario demonstrates, as described below, how practices in programs of literacy for deaf children may be contributing to this failure. Although they are gradually changing, these practices, in some form, are common to many programs. The discussion also suggests how a developmental perspective might change these practices.

Practices That May Impede the Development of Literacy

Choosing (or designing) programs based on criteria other than a child's needs
Beginning with very young deaf children, parents and educators often make educational decisions that are not based primarily on the child's individual needs for development. For example, in the scenario, parents, possibly with the advice of educators, may have chosen a preschool program without taking into account the child's linguistic needs. Often there is a tendency to choose (or design) educational programs based on other criteria, including 1) someone else's recommendation, 2) the parents' wishes regardless of actual linguistic need, or 3) proximity to home. The assumption here is that a "good" early childhood program for deaf children *teaches* language, regardless of the method, designing activities, and lessons for this purpose. Some may also assume—and accept—the possibility that within this instructional process the rate of language development will be slower for deaf children than it is for hearing children. Others, however, may believe that the rate of development should be the same, *regardless of the match between the child's needs and the conditions of the program*, if the program is "good enough" and the placement early enough.

Those employing developmental practices for teaching literacy make decisions about placement and other instructional issues on the basis of the child's need. Knowledge of the maturational aspects of learning supports these decisions. For example, the assumption that language is taught does not reflect an understanding of how children learn language most efficiently—that is, they acquire it as the result of comprehensible input during the critical years of early childhood (Krashen, 1992). In the early childhood years, children (deaf or hearing) need to be able to use and understand language in routine, age-appropriate activities, such as group play. (This chapter discusses this process in more detail.) For hearing children, this happens naturally; for deaf children, one should make every effort possible to replicate these conditions in order to support normal, timely development. This involves determining, as early as possible, how an individual deaf child will access language (for most, this will be through vision), then building on that information to create conditions to provide the appropriate input. Matching conditions for acquiring language to the child's needs—in the educational community and in the home—is different from placing a child in a program because of reputation, proximity, or any other criteria.

There are milestones in the acquisition of conversational language that all children achieve, regardless of the language or language modality (visual or auditory) they use. The goal should be for deaf children in early childhood to achieve the conversational milestones indicated for that period of growth. During these years, educators should monitor the children's language development continuously according to these benchmarks of progress. Individual patterns that show a widening discrepancy in development compared with the benchmarks should raise questions about the accessibility and input of the language—the match between conditions and the child's needs—among potentially contributing factors. Too often educators, and parents, do not attribute a growing discrepancy between a deaf child's development of language and recognized stages of development to a program's mismatch with the child's linguistic needs *until the child has passed the critical years for optimal acquisition of language*.

Establishing instructional goals according to age or grade, regardless of development

A second characteristic of the scenario above that may impede literacy progress concerns educational planning that is guided primarily by grade level expectations. Often a program establishes goals in literacy according to age, grade, or curricula *without considering whether they are developmentally appropriate for the student*. Both deaf and hearing children reach "school" age (five or six years) with varying developmental patterns of strengths and instructional needs. The variations among deaf children, as a group, are even greater than are those among hearing children. Nevertheless, schools typically place these children in academic programs using commercial materials or district curricula that reflect assumptions about the skills, knowledge, and experiences that children have acquired by this age—assumptions about their previous development. The curricula focus on learning to read and write and then using these skills to learn. This flows from the extended assumption that all children are ready for this instruction. The program determines the objectives supporting these goals according to grade.

When these goals and objectives coincide with students' developmental needs, this approach may work to some degree. For many children, however, the ensuing instruction is not in tune with the individual's pattern of development, nor does it represent an accurate view of the learning process. When instruction proceeds from goals and objectives that do not match a child's developmental needs, it is likely to be less than effective, especially if this practice continues over time.

Teachers should guide instruction with assessment that examines patterns of development of literacy—both achievements and unmet needs—from previous stages of development as well as the present stage. Goals and objectives should be based on this information and seek to meet learning needs that are necessary to support additional growth. In other words, if a child did not learn certain skills, knowledge, or strategies in an earlier stage of development, and these are important to achieving the goals of the present stage, then teachers should target them for instruction. Instruction should not be guided by materials that are based on implicit assumptions about what students can and cannot do. Instead, teachers should assess each child's development to uncover this information and then use it to make instructional decisions and priorities. Drawing instructional goals from sources of curricular information without considering the individual's development is risky.

Caution should be used when basing instruction on individual needs. When teachers base instruction on individual needs, they should not lose sight of the milestones and timetable of normal development. It is easy to become complacent with the progress that children are making and not recognize a widening gap between that progress and expectations for normal development. Teachers must use the information about developmental stages to gauge patterns of individual progress and to challenge the effectiveness of the instruction and assessment in the classroom.

Narrowly defining the areas of learning within literacy development and separating them for instructional purposes

A third practice that impedes deaf children's progress is the tendency for educators to limit their view of literacy to students' competencies in reading and writing. Further damage is done by separating—with instruction and assessment—these interdependent areas of learning. Embedded in these practices is the tendency to overlook conversational language as a major component in the development of literacy, one that facilitates not only learning to read and write but also learning in all other areas. Programs rarely assess conversational language as a factor influencing deaf children's progress in reading. In many cases, once a deaf child is "school age" and can communicate socially, people ignore degree of language competence as a variable that could contribute to or hinder the child's development of literacy. Again, the hidden assumption in many elementary level commercial materials or district curricula is that the children have acquired proficiency in conversational language. This tendency to neglect the interdependency of literacy processes results in the failure to establish instruction that supports learning in one area with strengths in another.

Assessment and instruction should reflect a view of literacy that demonstrates the interrelated nature of the major processes involved: conversational language and written language (reading and writing). The procedures for record keeping should manifest this perspective as well; the *Primary Language Record* (Barrs, Ellis, Hester, & Thomas, 1989), described at length in Chapter 4, demonstrates one approach to this. This record keeping system documents progress in conversational language beyond the preschool years and records that progress as part of the development of literacy. In this way, the *Record* reflects the concept that a program should monitor these areas in the development of literacy interdependently. It reinforces the understanding that competency in conversational language affects achievement in reading and writing, as well as learning in all areas.

In summary, assessment should support instruction that is developmentally appropriate. Assessment should also examine the primary (but not exclusive) expressions of literate thought: conversation, reading, and writing. These areas are discussed below.

Conversational Language

Educators must establish the timely acquisition of conversational language as a goal for deaf children. This is one of the first milestones in the development of literacy, one that precedes the achievement of competency in written language. However, one must approach this goal with an understanding of what constitutes a language, how children learn it, and how to monitor it in the classroom. This section will point out that deaf children come to the task of learning language with the same equipment that hearing children do—an innate ability to acquire language. Given the same conditions for acquiring language that hearing children have (abundant, accessible language input through use), deaf children acquire language in the same time frame and according to the same milestones as their hearing peers (Meier, 1991; Petitto, 1994). The goal of early acquisition of language should override preferences of modality. The pressing concern should be, *What language will achieve the goal of early acquisition and how can the conditions for its use be facilitated?*

Defining Language

Languages include those that are spoken and signed. The underlying formation of different languages is the same. In his best seller, *The Language Instinct,* linguist Stephen Pinker (1994) builds a fascinating case for a theory first proposed by Noam Chomsky—that there is a common universal language underlying all languages. Pinker refers to this as "mentalese," an internal language resulting from the innate ability of all humans to map their understanding of the world into mental, grammatical-like categories. This internal language does not involve the specifics or detail of spoken or signed languages, but classifies aspects of experience as "noun-like" or "verb-like." In other words, the mind stores ideas in categories that mimic the basic syntactical components common to all languages. These categories evolve as individuals learn about objects and their relationships in the environment. People think in this "language of thought,"(p. 81) rather than in English, ASL, Japanese, German. This universal language ability predisposes children biologically to acquire the specifics of the language used in their environment. *Language, then, is not thought itself but the symbols imposed to represent concepts and the relationships between concepts—the mechanism that translates "mentalese" into strings of words, or signs, and visa versa* (Pinker, 1984, p. 82).

Specific languages arise out of the need individuals have to communicate with others. *The separateness of groups of people, the passing down of language from generation to generation, and innovation in languages (changes in languages over time, such as coining new words) are characteristics of languages.* However, as Pinker (1994) explains, there are no Stone Age languages, even though Stone Age societies may have existed (p. 27). All languages, no matter how primitive the society from which they arise, are equally sophisticated when measured according to grammatical complexity. Further, *dialects* within the same language are of equal sophistication. [This concept refutes the notion that dialects associated with a particular class or race (e.g., working class or Black English Vernacular) are inferior on the grounds that they do not comply with rules for "standard" English.] *Languages are considered grammatical as long as they are "well-formed according to consistent rules in the dialect of the speakers"*(p. 31). Languages and their dialects are the different ways in which groups of people code the same underlying patterns of "mentalese" in order to communicate with each other.

Languages have a great deal in common, sharing a system of syntactic, morphologic, and phonologic rules and principles, with a small set of "parameters" that describe their differences. In all cases they exhibit a pattern of two sets of rules: one for arranging phonemes into morphemes and one for arranging morphemes within words and phrases. The words in all languages have stable meanings as well.

The way languages are built is similar, too—words are grouped into phrases and phrases into sentences, for example. The sharing of the grammatical code of a language allows the community of speakers or signers to convey and understand linguistic messages (Pinker, 1994, p. 237). All languages can communicate abstract ideas that are remote from the speaker, or signer, in time and space.

These common features allow linguists to study languages comparatively and have led to the recognition that signed languages exhibit all of the known characteristics of spoken languages. Pinker (1994) acknowledges this in the following quote:

> *Contrary to popular misconceptions, sign languages are not pantomimes and gestures, inventions of educators, or ciphers of the spoken language of the surrounding community. They are found wherever there is a community of deaf people, and each one is a distinct, full language, using the same kinds of grammatical machinery found worldwide in spoken languages* (p. 36).

For example, the same basic components found in spoken languages have been identified in signed languages as follows:

Components of Language	Spoken English	American Sign Language
Syntax: Rules of grammar; the "design" of language [There are some general rules for phrase structure that apply to all languages]	Words arranged in phrases and sentences in speech—producing a linear arrangement of phrases	Signs representing the same basic form classes as spoken languages—nouns, pronouns, verbs, adjectives, and adverbs—appearing in a sequence, as in spoken languages, but with variable word order (Newport & Meier, 1985, p. 884)
Morphology: Rules for arranging smaller segments of meaning into words	Segments of meaning arranged linearly to compose words (inflections added to root words)	Morphological components simultaneously organized—morphemes embedded within one another, e.g., In verbs of motion (run, etc.) The handshape is one morpheme, the path of movement another (p. 884)
Phonology: Rules for arranging the forms of the language used to formulate words; the phonemes of a language are meaningless in themselves	Connected sounds in speech arranged to compose words, phrases, sentences [There are rules underlying the arrangement of these sounds, for example, certain sounds are never connected]	Parameters including hand configuration, place of articulation, and movement arranged to compose signs (p. 883) [There are also rules limiting the arrangement of these parameters (p. 883)]

Just as there are similarities among languages[2] there are, of course, differences. Languages differ in the specific configuration of features. Also, there is a difference between the channels used for spoken and signed languages (mouth to ear vs. hand to eye). "Although we are biologically equipped to use language, we are not biologically limited to speech" (Meier, 1991, p. 60).

Acquiring Language vs. "Learning" Language

Language is most effectively and efficiently acquired rather than taught. Krashen (1992) distinguishes between *learning* a language, a conscious process associated with instruction, drill, and practice, and *acquiring* one, an unconscious process. He explains that under normal conditions, we acquire the vast majority of our language and draw from this source unconsciously when we produce language. We often use the part we learn to consciously "monitor," or correct, what we say or sign. Krashen further explains that we acquire language through "comprehensible input" (p. 4)—being surrounded by language that is understandable to us. In other words, access to comprehensible input is one of the conditions of acquiring language.

Krashen's theories fit neatly with Pinker's discussion of how individuals are "wired" to acquire the language of their environment. Having internal representations of thought that form the rudiments of language categories prepares infants to develop a specific language through observing its use. In other words, as infants observe the ways that others use language with them and in their environment, they internally define the specifics of a language as it fits with their mentalese, their internal categories of thought. Pinker (1994) says that *observation of language in use* is more responsible for acquisition than feedback or practice. In fact, practice may be superfluous to learning grammar (p. 279). Observing alone is not enough, however. Pinker gives the example of deaf parents of hearing children who, at times, have been encouraged to have their children watch a lot of television in order to facilitate the acquisition of spoken English. In no case did the children learn English. The speakers were remote, and the topics unrelated to their experience (p. 278). Children need "comprehensible input"—language used in the here-and-now, connected to shared experiences.

---

[2] Signed languages, such as ASL, are recognized as natural languages because they conform to the definitions of language discussed. There is general scientific agreement, however, that invented sign-based systems (e.g., Signing Exact English) used as educational tools with deaf children are not "real" or natural languages because they do not conform to these definitions. Further, there is evidence that the brain's processing of these systems differs from its processing of natural languages, signed or spoken (Petitto, 1993).

During the process of acquisition, hearing children pass through a series of recognized stages of language development at roughly the same ages (e.g., see descriptions in Hoskisson & Tompkins, 1987; Gleason, 1993). These stages of development, and their characteristic milestones, define "normal" development, even though it is accepted that children may differ by as much as a year or more within this pattern of normal development (Pinker, 1994). Deaf children's development of language using ASL under conditions similar to those for hearing children (the same amount and kind of exposure to the use of language during critical years) compares to these stages as well. Studies have determined that deaf children using ASL in conditions comparable to those for hearing children pass through these same stages at the same ages (Meier, 1991; Petitto, 1994). This observation gives additional weight to the usefulness of assessing deaf children's language according to stages of development.

The Timing of Language

In addition to the characteristics of each stage, the *timing* of development—a subject Pinker (1994) treats at length—has special implications for deaf education. He attributes the fact that language develops when it does, predominantly in the first few years of childhood, to conditions and changes in brain development. In other words, Pinker suggests that language is on a developmental timetable, like teeth (p. 289). He uses studies of individuals introduced to a new language at different ages to show how *normal* language development (the unconscious, acquisitional process leading to native fluency that occurs the early years of life) seems to be a function of brain capacity. He asserts that this capacity is "guaranteed for children up to the age of six, becomes progressively compromised thereafter until shortly after puberty, and is rare thereafter" (p. 293; Long, 1990). In other words, after age six, children acquire language with far more effort and rarely demonstrate native fluency. Typically, instruction must support acquisition beyond this point. Deaf people who have not been exposed to sign language until they are adults never do as well as those who learned it as young children (p. 291). Pinker asserts that the capacity to *acquire* language (not the ability to use it) has evolved to disappear after a certain age because it is no longer needed—the brain's energies naturally shift to other issues of development. Tying this together with what we know about languages, how people acquire them, and the fact that they can be signed or spoken, leads to the following implications for the programming and assessment of language development with deaf children:

> ▶ Deaf children should enter early childhood programs that will foster the *acquisition* of language as much as possible. In order for this to happen, the language input must be comprehensible—input the child can observe, understand, and use naturally. In other words, the language must match the child's sensory abilities—be accessible. The

language used must be represented in full detail. In other words, those involved with the child must use a true language that is clearly and fully represented.

▶ Adults should make every effort to create the conditions for acquisition as early as possible in order to maximize the critical period of learning language.

▶ Adults should monitor the child's language continuously according to known stages of development, comparing individual patterns of growth with these benchmarks of progress. Significant and increasing distinctions between a child's pattern of development and the recognized milestones of development indicate the need for more extensive evaluation of the conditions (including the choice of language used), the child, and the match between the two.

The Relationship of Conversational Language to Further Development of Literacy

Developing conversational language is a goal in itself. It is also, however, an important part of the development of one's literacy. There are two interdependent ways in which competency in conversational language prepares children for further development of literacy. One concerns the growth of world knowledge that children acquire through social interaction. The other is related to the acquisition of a language.

Competency in conversational language enables one to "parse" incoming information for meaning (Pinker, 1994). When people converse in a shared language, the receiver makes rapid decisions about meaning as incoming information automatically filters through an internalized language system: knowledge of the phonology, morphology, and syntax of the language. "Parsing" is used both in conversation and with text, e.g., in reading.

Conversational language, then, is one of the ways in which we receive information—one of the ways we acquire world knowledge. For those who do not read or do not read well, it is the primary (but not exclusive) way they receive information. A well-developed language system—plus opportunities to use it in rich, meaningful activities—facilitates learning. Conversely, a poorly developed language system, coupled with fewer opportunities to use it, deprives children of a source of information.

World knowledge promotes learning in all areas, including literacy. It enhances children's potential to build on what they know (increase their knowledge), to learn to think critically, and to develop the capability to reason abstractly (Bruce & Davidson, 1994). Applied to literacy, this area of development—the ability to think critically and reflectively—does not, and should not, depend upon knowing how to read and write (Paul, 1998). World knowledge evolves out of conversational language, beginning when children are young, and should continue to be learned conversationally. Reading and writing are but one source of this information.

For deaf children (indeed, all children), the acquisition of world knowledge depends upon the timely acquisition of conversational language. (This chapter previously discussed the conditions for acquiring language.) As noted, too, the development of world knowledge depends upon children's having opportunities to use conversational language with others in varied, meaningful experiences. Learning and sharing conversational language *in early childhood* are more likely to prepare deaf children for further academic development than other factors. Also, this is likely to be true regardless of whether the conversational language is the same language in which the children will be expected to read and write. For example, deaf children of deaf parents typically reach higher levels of academic achievement than deaf children of hearing parents (see discussion in Israelite et al., 1989). Doubtless one of the primary reasons for this is that they develop conversational language and world knowledge in ways that are similar to hearing children—at an early age and through social interaction in meaningful activities.

World knowledge facilitates learning to read and write as children begin to apply what they know about different topics to comprehend and produce text. Those who have varied and extensive background knowledge are better prepared than are those with less, or inaccurate, background knowledge. The more one knows about a given subject, the easier it is to understand written text. Recommendations are often made to begin reading instruction with "language experience" stories—texts written about children's experiences—for that reason (Weaver, 1988). These activities aim at providing the closest match possible between the text and what a child knows.

An internalized knowledge of language, developed through conversation, also prepares children to learn to read and write. Hearing children who speak the same language they read have internalized knowledge that helps them parse the text (Pinker, 1994). Basically, they learn to use the same information with which they parse conversation to help comprehend written language: their knowledge of phonology, morphology, syntax, and the meanings of words. In order to read, they must learn to apply this knowledge and their world knowledge in order to comprehend information in print. Deaf children who develop a natural signed language internalize a system that is different from the one in text. However, if they are competent in this conversational language and have sufficient background knowledge, they are prepared to learn to read and write as developmentally indicated. The approach to their instruction, however, will be different from the approach one uses with their hearing peers.

Deaf children do not acquire knowledge of written language conversationally, as hearing children do, having limited (or no) auditory access to the spoken form of the language. Furthermore, they usually fail to learn the written language through the various sign systems developed for this purpose (Hoffmeister, 1992; Hoffmeister and Bahan, 1991; Livingston, 1983; Marmor and Petitto, 1979; Maxwell, 1987; Supalla, 1986; Svartholm. 1993.) However, deaf children do need to develop a working knowledge of written language in order to parse sentences in text. The challenge is how to help them acquire or learn that knowledge. In other words, how can one make the language in which text is written more accessible to them? This happens to some degree, for some individuals, naturally through extensive reading and early experiences in literacy. Opportunities for this kind of learning need to be increased. For many deaf children, however, this will continue to be a matter of instruction.

What is important *not* to do, however, is to try to develop deaf children's knowledge of written language through such instruction at the expense of developing their competency in conversation and world knowledge. This happens often and in many ways, and it leaves children ill-prepared for further development in two ways: they have inadequate and delayed development in conversational language, and they are lacking in background knowledge. These children are not prepared to learn to read and write or to further their development of literacy through conversation.

For this reason, many educators of deaf children are emphasizing the importance of the children developing competency in conversational language (and world knowledge) before they are taught *formally* to read and write (e.g., Johnson et al, 1989). Since many feel it is difficult to predict a very young deaf child's proclivity for understanding and expressing spoken language, they advocate achieving early conversational competence with a signed language—ASL—because of its visual accessibility to deaf children. ASL, then, becomes these children's first language and a tool to make their world comprehensible.

Consequently, these children learn to read and write English as a second language. Those who support this approach emphasize that children should be surrounded by meaningful, enjoyable experiences with text from an early age, but that formal teaching of reading and writing should not be undertaken until they have acquired a high degree of proficiency in the first language (Cummins and Swain, 1986)). They also stress the importance of maintaining the first language (ASL) in order to further literacy development and learning in all areas (Mahshie, 1995; Collier, 1989, 1994 as cited in Mahshie, 1995).

Advocates of this approach maintain that students need to be able to use conversational language for *academic purposes* before formal instruction in reading and writing, introduced with a second language, can succeed (Cummins, 1981, as cited in Mahshie, 1995). In other words, children should be able to use conversational language to discuss abstract concepts that have very little contextual support. A child with good conversational skills in a contextually rich environment (familiar people, shared experiences, concrete social interactions) may be assumed to have a higher level of linguistic ability than he or she actually does. The danger in this assumption is that the child may not have the deeper competency in language he or she needs to cope with academic demands.

In summary, proficiency in conversational language prepares children for further development in literacy and all areas of learning. It does so by facilitating the development of world knowledge and the knowledge of language. Children should continue to learn world knowledge and related critical thinking through conversation and with multiple sources of information at all levels of development. Most deaf children achieve these goals best with a visual language.

Reading and Writing

As stated earlier, conversation is one way of communicating thoughts and information; reading and writing are other ways used in our society. Although different cultures place different values on competencies in literacy, such as reading and writing, it is an inescapable fact that knowing how to read and write better equips individuals, deaf or hearing, to function in today's society. In order to support the suggestions in this chapter and the next for assessing these competencies, the background information following here discusses the nature of these processes.

Reading

The most widely accepted model of reading is an interactive model (Stanovich, 1980; see discussions in Garner, 1987; Paul, 1998). It further defines the reading process described by previous models, the bottom-up and the top-down models. The bottom-up models, the more traditional of these two, represent reading as the culmination of a series of skills that, once learned, enable one to read.

Bottom-up models focus on the text itself—on what the reader can learn from it, beginning with its smallest units, the alphabet and phonetic information, and working up to larger pieces of information, or connected text. Top-down models, developed largely in reaction to this traditional concept, emphasize the reader aspects of the reading, or personal background knowledge, including language. According to these models, reading is a top-down process of determining meaning based on the information one brings to the task. Top-down models propose that reading is a process of sampling the text (not reading every word), making predictions about meaning, and looking for confirmations by reading further in order to obtain meaning from print. Further, top-down models indicate that the process does not depend upon the prior learning of smaller skills in isolation.

An interactive model describes reading as a task that involves both top-down and bottom-up processing—using features of text, the printed language, as well as background knowledge. This model indicates that reading uses both processes and that the balance of use depends upon many variables, including the demands of the task (e.g., degree of familiarity with topic). However, this model does not describe the use of these processes as unilateral (top-down or bottom-up); instead it indicates that reading involves the "simultaneous application of multiple knowledge sources" (Rumelhart, as cited in Garner, 1987, p. 3). An important, related theory in this model is that one different strategy, or skill, (e.g., bottom-up, such as decoding, vs. top-down, such as applying prior knowledge) may compensate for another. For example, a skillful decoder may be able to understand a difficult text even though he or she lacks prior knowledge of the subject.

The interactive model of reading is supported by theories of learning similar to those discussed in Chapter 1. They include the following (see discussion in Shanklin and Rhodes, 1993).

▶ Reading must be learned as a constructive mental process—readers must learn to apply what they know.

▶ Readers must develop background knowledge (world and linguistic knowledge) and learn to apply this, as indicated above, to the reading task.

▶ There are strong social aspects to reading and learning to read—reading is learned, and should be taught, socially.

Readers must learn to actively construct meaning from text by applying what they know to the task. In other words, they are not passive recipients of information that lies exclusively in the print. An example of this constructive mental process involves the reader's application of cue systems (language knowledge) as a means to comprehending text (e.g., Goodman, Watson, & Burke, 1987). These cue systems are linguistic and include one's knowledge of graphophonics (relationships of letters to sounds), semantics (the meanings of words), and syntax (the structure of language). In addition to this linguistic information, readers must learn to apply what they know about the subject and to use strategies for comprehension—ways to monitor and correct their understanding.

Students' background knowledge (what they already know) is organized in a schema (Anderson & Pearson, 1984). One's schema is used to relate and learn new information. It is the old information, organized in mental categories (schema), that leads individuals to have certain expectations about incoming information. This enables one to make predictions. The more the new information fits with one's expectations (confirms predictions), the more easily one understands it. A schema—what one already knows—facilitates reading comprehension to the degree that it is complete, accurate, and used actively during the reading process. The active use of one's schema involves reflective thinking.

The social aspect of learning to read is a critical component in the development of literacy and is linked to motivation—another component (Paris, Wasik, & Turner, 1991). For example, children learn early behaviors concerning reading through interactions with others, both in the home and at school. Whether or not we are read to as children, or observe others reading, has a powerful effect on what we learn as well as what we deem is important to learn. Our conversations with others in activities related to literacy tend to scaffold us to higher levels of understanding, both of concepts within the text and strategies used to interpret the meaning. Our attitudes and cultural expectations, which we develop through social interactions, affect our progress in learning to read by determining what we establish as personal goals for learning. Our personal goals motivate us to learn.

Deaf Children and Reading

As pointed out by Paul (1998), the process of reading (and learning to read) for most deaf children is both similar to and different from the process most hearing children experience. For example, deaf children apply both bottom-up and top-down skills and strategies in reading, as indicated with the interactive model of reading. They also learn to read according to the theories listed above: actively applying a constructive process, using schema, and engaging in social interaction. The difference, however, is in the linguistic experiences and knowledge that many deaf children bring to these processes. Some of these children—those who have proficiency in ASL—may bring comparable experiences and knowledge, but these are not based on the same language in the text. Their internalized language system is different from the cue systems applied to reading English. Also, the experiences stored in their memory are schematically different from those of children whose experiences are associated with English vocabulary. These deaf children may come to reading with competencies and knowledge that are age-appropriate but different from those used by hearing readers who experience print having acquired the same language communicatively. Deaf children in this case are learning to read in a second language, ASL being the first. They must still develop a working knowledge of English in order to read.

Many other deaf children, however, come to the task of learning to read and write while still in the process of developing linguistic experiences and knowledge that are usually acquired in early childhood. They also may have differences between the language they use for conversation and the one they use for print, but their more critical differences are in the degree to which they have developed linguistic experiences and knowledge. For these children, assessment of their literacy should guide instruction to focus on developing linguistic experiences and related conceptual knowledge. As discussed in the introduction to this chapter, there is a tendency to isolate instruction in reading and writing from conversational language goals when deaf children reach a certain age. This practice perpetuates a remedial approach (Johnston & Allington, 1991) to teaching reading (e.g., approaching problems in learning to read and write as deficiencies in these tasks) rather than a developmental approach. Teachers need information about the other variables related to the development of literacy— not just progress in reading and writing—to determine the instructional needs of these children adequately.

Writing

In recent years educators have more frequently discussed writing in relation to reading; they often refer to the two as complements of one another (e.g., Graves, 1991; Hoskisson & Tompkins, 1987). The task of writing involves the same interactive processes used in reading, including both bottom-up and top-down skills and strategies. Also, the same theories of learning described for reading apply to writing. In addition to these theories, Krashen (1992) proposes that children learn writing more through reading than through writing. The reason for this, he explains, is that reading provides the comprehensible input about print that they use in writing. Reading can facilitate the acquisition of far more knowledge (e.g., about language, conventions, spelling, vocabulary, etc.) than children can learn through instruction.

Traditionally, people have discussed writing in relation to language, however. The focus on ability in and knowledge of the English language has been a prominent feature in the traditional views of writing and how it has been taught—for deaf and hearing children. Instruction and assessment arising from this perspective have centered on the product of writing and how well it reflects correct, or standard, use of language, measuring proficiency in writing according to this standard. Thus educators with this perspective have taught writing almost exclusively via lessons in the skills of language—grammar, spelling, punctuation—a practice that has proved to have little effect in improving writing ability for any group of children (Krashen, 1992). Instruction in these skills is most effective when it occurs as developmentally needed and in the context of genuine writing tasks. Further, this view of writing—one that is grounded in the skills of language—has perpetuated the focus of writing instruction on lower-level, text-based skills, while neglecting the top-down skills and strategies that are equally important to the task.

The interactive model of reading and the more recent theories about learning to read and write (constructive processing, use of schema, and others) are responsible for the changing views on writing. As with reading, more recent views of writing account for both bottom-up, surface level text skills (such as spelling, grammar, punctuation) and higher level, more complex thinking skills, (such as organization, style, sense of audience). Also, studies of how proficient writers approach writing have resulted in an understanding of the task as something that involves multiple steps. The act of effectively incorporating both bottom-up and top-down skills and strategies in print is often carried out in a series of writing activities. In fact, good writers are distinguished more for the strategies they use to develop the text (higher level thinking skills) than for their proficiency in English language skills. According to Krashen (1992), good writers take more time to think about what they want to write before putting pencil to paper; they are more reflective. They re-scan as they write, pausing frequently and rereading what they have put down. Also, they revise with a focus on clarifying meaning, rather than focusing on sentence-level, mechanical errors as poor writers do. Poor writers, deaf or hearing, may have difficulties with the language, but they are distinguished as well by their inability to apply good strategies to the writing task.

These studies have given rise to a process approach to teaching writing, one that involves developing text through planning, composing, and revising (Alden & Foss-Lundin, 1994; Paul, 1998). Teaching and assessing writing this way, the *process* involved in the development of written work—including both top-down and bottom-up skills applied in this process—becomes as much a focus of instruction as the completed, written product. Also, the strategies used in this process become a source of instructional information. Students are taught to reflect more on their writing throughout the process and bottom-up skills are taught in the context of developing the text. Children—deaf and hearing—have benefited from the application of a process approach to teaching writing. By recognizing the multiple tasks involved in writing, and separating them when approaching the task, a more accurate, natural approach to instruction has evolved. This approach, too, supports the social aspect of learning in that it recognizes the importance of feedback to the learning process.

Deaf Children and Writing

For deaf children, learning to write is both similar to and different from the way hearing children learn this task, and for many of the same reasons described for reading. As with reading, most deaf children who come to the task of writing have different linguistic knowledge than hearing children who are learning to write in the same language they have acquired conversationally. As with reading, these differences may be in the kinds of language (having a conversational language that is different from the written language), the degree of competence in the conversational language, or both. Again, it is important to assess their competencies as descriptively as possible for instructional planning.

Instruction in writing for deaf children also should focus on the changes in perspective described above. These children should be taught with a process approach and with an emphasis on the learning strategies that good writers use—planning, re-scanning, and revising for meaning. Learning and using these strategies will require that they become more reflective about their writing. Also, these children should be taught language and mechanical skills as developmentally needed and in the context of genuine writing tasks. Finally, teachers should recognize the relationship between writing and reading, and understand that reading—more than practice in writing—has a stronger influence on improving progress in this area.

Implications: Characteristics of Developmental Literacy Programs

The preceding discussions about conversational language and written language—reading and writing—provide information about desired characteristics of literacy programs of deaf children.

In essence, these programs would approach the development of deaf children's literacy holistically and developmentally and they would be different from those depicted in the introductory scenario. Teachers would make decisions about planning for literacy based on the child's needs and individual development (Johnston, 1984). They would examine multiple variables, not just reading and writing, as part of that process. Progress would be monitored and recorded with this same perspective over time—according to how multiple variables influence development interdependently. Assessment and instruction would use information about established stages of development through which all children proceed to determine individual patterns and needs.

Early Childhood

Based on what is known about conversational language, a program would establish goals for children to acquire competence in conversational language during early childhood. The approach to this would involve determining the child's linguistic needs—ascertaining which language is accessible and creating social conditions that foster its acquisition. (For some children, this means providing sufficient access to both spoken and signed language in different contexts.) Further, children would engage in varied and rich experiences as they are developing conversational language so that they could acquire world knowledge as well. These experiences would also include natural interactions with others related to print (being read to, talking about lists for shopping, noticing environmental signs, etc.).

Curricular Content

When children became competent users of conversational language and developmentally ready in other ways, they would begin more formal schooling. Teachers would establish educational goals, again, according to individual need. These goals would address what children should learn next according to information in different curricular areas. Reading and writing would not be the focus of children's programming, nor would these skills be the primary way in which children receive and communicate information. Conversation (using the language the child develops), videotapes, and class experiences, for example, would provide rich contexts for learning. In other words, programs for instruction in reading and writing would be well developed but not separate from, or the gateway to, what children learn of content information. Formal academic instruction in literacy and other areas would extend the use of conversational language as a means for acquiring information and for developing reflective, critical thinking skills.

Literacy Instruction

Children would learn reading and writing in this context—as one of the ways to receive and communicate information. Instruction in reading and writing would take into consideration a number of factors: the degree of competency in conversational language, whether learning to read and write is taking place in the child's first language or in a second or other language, and the ways in which motivation and social interactions influence—or could be used to influence—the learning process. Instruction would focus on helping students develop the background knowledge they need for reading and writing— knowledge about language, the world, and strategies they could use in print tasks. Students would be taught with a strong emphasis on reflective thinking about their knowledge.

Assessment

Assessment in the classroom in these programs would follow suit. Teachers would monitor conversational language according to normal patterns of development. This would continue until the children attained mature, academic levels of use. Further, when students began to learn to read and write, teachers would monitor their proficiency in conversational language as part of their progress in these areas. Assessment would also consider other factors, such as motivation and social interactions.

Assessment approached this way would serve two purposes. One purpose would be to monitor progress in the multiple variables in the development of literacy (conversational and written language, social interactions, and motivation) over time, within the framework of normal development. This would enable those involved to plan and adjust long-term instructional goals aimed at the balance of these variables. The framework of stages of development would be used to interpret individual patterns of growth and to maintain a view of these patterns with respect to the milestones and timetable of normal development.

The long-term goals the program establishes for children with this framework would provide the context for assessment serving the second purpose: assessment that measures day-to-day progress in learning, according to the variables defined in literacy. Assessment that serves this purpose involves multiple methods, examines many types of learning, and is as descriptive as possible of students' strengths and instructional needs. It must be conducted in partnership with others, especially the students themselves. Further, the procedures must also examine progress over time and be capable of encapsulating that progress within the larger framework of development.

The next section discusses a tool designed to support the first of these purposes—to establish long-term goals. Assessment for the second purpose is treated in more detail in the following chapter.

Stages of Literacy Development

To establish long-term goals, teachers need a system for putting information about students into a longitudinal framework—a profile of literacy development. A model framework designed for this purpose—to guide and interpret assessment in the classroom developmentally—is discussed in this section. The proposed tool is a continuum of stages in the development of literacy designed to facilitate examining patterns of individual growth, over time, according to multiple areas of development. The Stages of Literacy Development, which are included in **Appendix A,** have two components:

- components of literacy, and

- stages of development.

Components of Literacy

The components, or areas of development, of literacy are either directly observable in the performance of a task, or they are areas of learning that can be inferred from students' behavior, discussions, and products of their work. Many of the components have been mentioned previously in parts of this or the first chapter, specifically in the sections about learning theory (Chapter 1) and the development of language, reading, and writing (this chapter). Others were identified by separating out, for the purposes of assessment, competencies that underlie more observable skills. The eight components include:

Communicative Competency: In the classroom, teachers should monitor conversational language by observing its use in different contexts—in other words, by observing a child's communicative competency. Knowledge of the language used by the child (e.g., the structure of that language) as well as information about stages of language development and behaviors associated with each should guide these observations. To support monitoring communicative competency, a rating scale developed for the Kendall Demonstration Elementary School, Gallaudet University (part of the Pre-College National Mission Programs) is included in the Stages. This scale, The Kendall Conversational Proficiency Levels, or "P-Levels," is included in **Appendix B**. The scale guides teachers to focus on the language competencies associated with different levels of development. Although the scale was originally designed exclusively as a tool for assessing communicative competency informally in the classroom, its use in this context also supports a holistic view of the development of literacy.

Motivation: Motivation is the outgrowth of affective variables at work in learning. The importance of these variables to the development of literacy was suggested in the discussions about learning theory presented in Chapter 1. Krashen's hypothesis of an *affective filter* at work in learning (1992, p.6) also explains the powerful influence of this component. He claims that a negative affective filter, created by such things as anxiety, low self-esteem, and negative beliefs about performance, prevents students from learning regardless of the appropriateness and quality of instruction. On the other hand, when this negative filter is lowered—when students are confident they can learn a targeted skill—motivation is heightened and this facilitates learning. In other words, motivation—or its absence due to negative feelings and personal beliefs about learning—influences learning as much as instruction.

Text Knowledge and Comprehension Strategies: This component includes the abilities that underlie reading comprehension. It is the component that most represents the targets of traditional assessment. However, in the Stages this component is designed to reflect an interactive model of the reading process, thus representing both bottom-up as well as top-down processing skills and strategies. These range from understanding the uses of print and knowing the names of letters to being able to apply effective comprehension strategies, such as locating the main ideas in written texts. It is important for educators to understand that this component and the "Forms of Writing" discussed later— the areas most typically targeted for instruction and assessment—do not and cannot develop in a vacuum apart from the others.

Background Knowledge: The importance of background knowledge relates to the concept of schema and its role in learning. As indicated earlier, one's prior learning, organized schematically in long-term memory, largely determines the ease with which one learns new information. For example, familiarity with concepts in the text greatly enhances comprehension in reading. Background knowledge includes not only experiential (topical) knowledge but also linguistic knowledge, including what students know about the language or languages they use.

Social Interactions: This component comes from the theory that learning develops through social interaction. As described earlier, conversation, reading, and writing are all ways of communicating thoughts and ideas to others, not end goals of instruction. Effective instruction must approach the development of literacy with authentic, collaborative activities that involve the purposeful use of language, reading, and writing. Establishing social interactions as one of the components of assessment reminds educators of the importance of this variable to development. Further, it prompts educators to observe how students engage in interaction with others—the degree of their interactions and the nature of these interactions—which can greatly influence learning.

Concepts of Print: This component represents what students appear to understand conceptually about writing by talking with them, observing them as they write, and examining their finished work. For example, young children will "play" with writing before they can actually write, pretending to make lists, send letters, and leave messages. This behavior indicates their growing understanding of the uses of writing. As students grow older, their ability to write for different purposes indicates their understanding of these purposes and the forms of each. Students also demonstrate understanding of specific skills used in writing, such as awareness of correct spelling, punctuation, etc. However, this component—conceptual understanding—was separated out from the more obvious writing components, such as the "forms" of writing and the process skills themselves, for a reason. It is possible for students to understand concepts about writing but not be able to implement them correctly. They may also not understand a concept important to a task or skill they are expected to perform.

Forms of Print: This component represents what teachers traditionally assess in writing—the end product of writing, or what is observable on the paper. Assessment of this component includes skills and concepts a child knows because they are demonstrated in use. However, as indicated with the previous component, it does not take into account those that a child may understand but not yet be able to demonstrate. There is a developmental progression in this component, just as there is in each of the others. Understanding that progression should help educators know what to expect of children at different levels and therefore what is reasonable to teach them.

Skills in the Writing Process: These skills, discussed earlier in the section about the writing process, have also been described developmentally, based on observations of the changes in children's writing over time. Children at different ages and points in development approach the steps in the writing process differently. This component helps teachers understand the maturational aspects of the writing process and emphasizes the importance of teaching students with this approach. Further, this component reinforces the need for students to develop the strategies that distinguish good and poor writers, such as planning, re-scanning, and revising for meaning.

In summary, these different components of literacy should be recognized through assessment and instruction. Sweet (1993, p. 4) defines literacy as a "myriad of factors related to the context of literacy activities (the type of activities) and the child's personal attributes, including cognitive development."

Assessment that examines various components of literacy is more consistent with this definition than traditional assessment, which has tended to focus on the products of reading and writing. In creating the Stages of Literacy Development, the goal was to couple the information about these components of literacy with identifiable stages in the development of literacy.

The Stages

The Stages of Literacy Development, including the sequence of these stages and the major tasks of achievement in each, comes largely from what is known about the developmental milestones of conversational language, reading, and writing (for hearing and deaf children) as they tend to occur given optimal conditions (e.g., Chall, 1983; Leslie, 1993; Meier, 1991; O'Donnell & Wood, 1992). The approximate timing of these stages is also noted. However, *the timing of developmental stages does not indicate when skills and strategies should be taught*. It is provided to further understand individual patterns of development—discrepancies in development, if they exist, among different components as well as discrepancies according to age. It is the pattern of this *combined* information—a child's age and the development of different components—that determines instructional direction. The stages of development for first language literacy include:

Emerging Literacy [Typical Age/Grade Levels: Birth-Kindergarten]
Acquiring conversational language and conceptual knowledge through experience and social interaction is the major task of development at this stage. However, foundations for progress in other components of literacy are also established during this stage. For example, motivation and conceptual understandings about print begin to form at this stage of development. Children grow in their understanding of literacy from their observations of others, their own experiences, and what they learn from exposure to society (media, signs, and other sources).

Beginning Literacy [Typical Grade Levels: Kindergarten-Grades 1, 2]
Students who have progressed to this level are becoming curious about the details of print—identifying commonly used words in the environment and developing strategies that will enable them to read and write. By the end of this stage, they begin to apply knowledge about language and the world around them to figure out printed text; and they should be able to read easy, predictable books. They also learn to express thoughts in writing using invented and conventional spellings and simple sentences.

Developing Literacy [Typical Grade Levels: Grades 2, 3, 4]
Students who have progressed to this level should begin to read and write extensively. Their task is to develop fluency. Students at this level should dramatically increase the number of words they recognize automatically in print and demonstrate a balanced use of cue systems in their reading. In their writing they develop control over the process of putting their ideas in print.

Maturing Literacy [Typical Grade Levels: Grades 4-6, 7, 8]
Students at this level increasingly use reading and writing as a means of learning. They read content material competently, and they express their thoughts in writing more and more succinctly. They continue to expand their reading vocabularies, understand material of increasing complexity, and learn to use productive strategies for study. These students read (and write) widely, both expository material and a variety of literary genre. Their cognitive development eventually takes them to a more sophisticated level of abstract reasoning about what they read and write.

Organization of the Stages of Literacy Development

In the Stages of Literacy Development, the components are listed according to the stages. In other words, the skills, strategies, and behaviors associated with each component are described at each stage, as illustrated below.

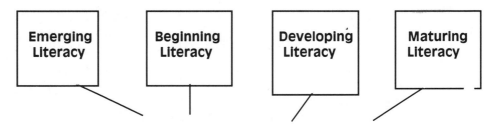

Includes skills, knowledge, behaviors within the following areas:

- Communicative Competency

- Motivation

- Text Knowledge/Comprehension Strategies

- Background Knowledge

- Social Interactions

- Concepts about Print

- Forms of Print

- Skills in the Writing Process

These skills, strategies, and behaviors are written as lists in **Appendix A**, as shown in the following excerpt from the stage called Emerging Literacy:

| **Emerging Literacy**

Text Knowledge/Reading Comprehension Strategies

⬛ identifies "who" and "what" in a story

⬛ can retell a familiar story with pictures after repeated listening

⬛ has some understanding of conventions of print (how books and print work)*

⬛ indicates comprehension of appropriate stories read aloud (with sign or speech) *

*See **Appendix C**: Early Reading Checklist | ↩ *Headings*: stage, or level, of development
↩ *Subheadings*: component, or area of development

↩ *Items with blanks*: competencies within the area of development
(May be marked with:
C = Consistently demonstrates,
A = Attempts to demonstrate, or
N = Needs to learn (add the "N" later when defining short term goals)

↩ *Asterisk and appendix*: notes assessment tools found in other appendices that may help a teacher assess selected competencies |

The goal for developing the Stages of Literacy Development was to provide information about key features of learning associated with each stage—data that would help teachers determine a child's level (and the nature) of development according to the different components. In other words, *the behaviors listed at different stages of development do not represent an inclusive, sequential list of skills that should be taught at each level—rather, they provide a snapshot of normal development at that stage.* The complete lists of Stages of Literacy Development are included in **Appendix A**.

Application of the Stages of Literacy Development

The Stages provide information about the maturation of various components of literacy based on tendencies of growth associated with normal development for hearing and deaf children. Teachers should use them, or a similar tool, to understand individual development and to establish long-term goals for instruction according to that understanding (also see **Appendix A-1**). They should not use them to determine instructional goals according to age, unless these coincide with those indicated by the child's actual development. In summary, teachers should use the Stages of Literacy Development to:

▶ **Determine the child's level of development.** This will be clearly indicated if all components are progressing simultaneously. In many cases, however, one may need to determine this by establishing the predominant level of development indicated by the various components within each stage.

▶ **Examine the relationship of development among components.** Are some components developing ahead of others? It is important to identify relationships among components at given points in time (e.g., at the end of each instructional year) as well as look for patterns of development among components over time. For example, the Stages could indicate that a child has lacked motivation, or development in other competencies, for several years. They could also indicate areas of competency that are strengths—those that appear to facilitate development in other areas.

▶ **Determine the primary focus of programming for literacy according to these patterns.** If a child is consistent in development across components, then planning focuses on furthering development within that level or to the next level. However, if there are discrepancies in development among components, planning must address these differences, setting goals for learning at different stages of development. Increasing motivation would become a long-term instructional goal for the child mentioned above.

▶ **Identify skills, strategies, and behaviors within components that need to be maintained or learned at a specific level of development.** This information should be the starting point for establishing short-term instructional goals according to need. If students already possess these skills, strategies, or behaviors, they do not need instruction in them.

Interpretation of a child's development with the Stages would involve knowing a child over time. For that reason, the Stages should be used at the close of an instructional year to summarize development and to indicate future needs. As previously mentioned, a variety of kinds of assessment data from multiple sources must contribute to this determination of a child's developmental progress. Tools used for this purpose, described in the next chapter, would contribute throughout the year to determining progress within the components.

Conclusion

Literacy develops as growth in many related areas, representing different kinds of knowledge. Teachers should assess it accordingly, with procedures that examine progress in these areas according to stages of development. The Stages of Literacy Development in this chapter exemplify a framework for this kind of assessment and for carrying out the developmental concepts described earlier in the chapter. Teachers can use the Stages, or similar tools, to identify areas of literacy that need to be developed, as well as those that are strengths. This information should inform planning long-term goals for students. When assessment is approached this way, teachers examine the *interdependency* of different areas in literacy development. If used for the purposes listed above, the Stages, or similar tools, might redirect instructional practices that are currently failing to achieve literacy goals established for students.

Assessment in the Classroom

Authentic Assessment

A Broad, Comprehensive Approach to Assessment

Alternative Methods of Assessing Literacy

Using Assessment to Build a Picture of Long-Term
      Development

Conclusion

Chapter 3

Assessment in the Classroom: Monitoring Learning, Informing Instruction

Teachers should determine long-term instructional goals for students by examining individual patterns of strengths and needs according to stages of literacy development. This was explained in the previous chapter's discussion of the Stages of Literacy Development (found in **Appendix A**). For example, suppose a young child demonstrated age-appropriate competency in all the areas indicated on the Emerging Literacy level of the Stages. Long-term goals and instructional planning for this child would focus on guiding him or her in the tasks specified for the next stage, Beginning Literacy. Suppose, on the other hand, an older child were functioning at the Developing Level in many print-based tasks but not making progress because of unmet needs at previous levels in applying background knowledge to reading or in developing proficiency in communicative competency. Instructional planning for this child must serve to fulfill these previously unmet needs in addition to those associated with the current level of functioning. In fact, facilitating the child's progress in his or her areas of need at lower levels of development should take instructional priority.

Throughout the year, long-term goals should guide instruction and assessment in the classroom. Day-to-day assessment, the subject of this chapter, should reveal what children know and are ready to learn next according to these goals. This process should culminate with summaries of students' progress at the end of the year that redefine the long-term goals. Often, however, this does not happen. In many cases, teachers plan long term goals according to curriculum objectives (the school's, the district's, or commercial) without the support of a *comprehensive, descriptive* assessment of each child.

Classroom assessment procedures that are used to gather information about students' progress often fall short of providing data that will adequately describe instructional strengths and needs, and redefine long-term goals for the following year. There are several reasons why this typically happens, as explained below. These inadequacies (stated in bold) each lend themselves to a corollary that illustrates how assessment might be used more effectively to guide instruction.

Inadequacy: Assessment often does not provide enough information about the various types of learning that are part of the development of literacy.

For children of elementary age, assessment tends to focus on their performance in reading and writing rather than taking into account the range of competencies in literacy, including affect or face-to-face communicative competency. Assessment should address various types of knowledge in order to represent multiple areas of learning as indicated with the components of the Stages of Literacy Development. The type(s) of learning should be identified prior to assessment, as part of the instructional goal (McTighe & Ferrara, 1994; Popham, 1995). McTighe and Ferrara classify different kinds of learning outcomes (results of instruction) as follows:

- *declarative knowledge*: what students understand, including facts, concepts, principles, generalizations,

- *procedural/process knowledge*: what students do to solve problems and work through the tasks of literacy (skills, processes, and strategies), and

- *attitudes, values, and habits of mind*: how students are disposed to act (e.g., make personal choices, resolve to learn new information, etc.) (p. 10).

Popham (1995) also discusses different kinds of learning as the targets for assessment, classifying them according to:

- *cognitive* assessment targets, or those related to intellectual operations,

- *affective* targets, or those that represent values and attitudes, and

- *psychomotor* targets, or those that involve muscle skills (p. 81)

When different types of knowledge are not assessed in the classroom, a child's development is not evaluated fully, and planning cannot be effective.

Corollary: Assess the different types of learning that are part of literacy development—not just students' knowledge of print (e.g., all of the components of the Stages of Literacy Development, described in Chapter 2 and found in Appendix A).

Inadequacy: Traditional paper-and-pencil tasks (e.g., multiple choice, true-false, fill in the blank, etc.), prominently used methods to assess literacy, are ineffective for assessing some types of learning and inappropriate for evaluating others.

Paper-and-pencil tasks, used alone, are ineffective for monitoring certain types of learning, including children's knowledge of conversational language, their knowledge of procedure and process, and their ability to apply higher-level thinking skills to authentic tasks.

Further, the results of assessment based on these methods may be influenced by a child's developing, but not yet proficient, use of written English as a second language. Written tests require a certain level of competency in reading and writing and may rely on the psychomotor skill of handwriting. For children who are still developing these competencies (reading, writing, and handwriting), paper-and-pencil tests may not accurately reveal other kinds of knowledge. Thus, they may be especially inappropriate for children at the lower levels of literacy development and for those who are learning to read and write in a second language.

Assessment in the classroom should use a variety of kinds of methods and continue to apply descriptive, observational methods well beyond the preschool years (when they are more typically used). The variety of tools a teacher uses should ensure that the target of assessment—the type of learning—is monitored with an appropriate tool or procedure (McTighe & Ferrara, 1994). The tool or procedure should provide the maximum and most accurate information about a child's knowledge of the target. As previously mentioned, teachers should plan assessment prior to instruction to help clarify the goal. Further, they should use multiple tools to support and confirm their assessment-related decisions about a child's progress or needs (e.g., McTighe & Ferrara, 1994).

Corollary: Use different types of methods to assess different types of learning, emphasizing descriptive methods (alternative assessments), to inform instruction.

Inadequacy: Year-end summaries of progress frequently fail to describe the current year's progress within a developmental framework—one that facilitates understanding of patterns in the development of literacy over time and indicates which competencies a child needs to acquire next.

Summaries of progress for the year are often close-up views of progress (narrowly defined, as described above) that do not put the information back into a broader picture of development. They are snapshots of a child's performance at the end of the year, communicated with grades, narratives, or a combination of the two. They typically do not lead to interpretations of the information according to a longitudinal picture of development—one that would indicate priorities for learning according to developmental order. Further, these close-up views often vary according to teachers' paradigms about what is important to learn, teach, and assess. Even if teachers agree among themselves on what students should learn, they often differ about how they should teach and assess this information.

Corollary: Summarize progress by putting the information back into a longitudinal, developmental framework that establishes goals for instruction (e.g., the Stages of Literacy Development or a similar tool).

In summary, programs need tools that will help interpret a child's progress in literacy over time. These tools should indicate what is important to monitor (components in the development of literacy). The tools should also provide direction for what to teach individual children by specifying long-term goals— areas in the development of literacy to prioritize for instruction—as well as short-term goals—what is developmentally appropriate to teach within these areas. Both kinds of goals indicate *what* a child needs to learn in order to progress further.

How to assess literacy within this context is the subject of the remainder of this chapter, which discusses what tools to use and how to use them in the classroom throughout the instructional year. Methods and procedures should support the goals of assessment indicated in the corollaries above. They are more likely to do so if teachers choose them according to the principles described in Chapter 1. *It is especially important that assessment tools, procedures, and methods represent authentic approaches to tasks, resulting in practices that are broad and comprehensive.*

Authentic Assessment

Assessing "Real World" Tasks in "Real World" Activities

There are two common interpretations of "authentic assessment." One interpretation refers to the degree to which assessment evaluates "real world" tasks in the context of "real world" activities (e.g., Wiggins, as cited in McTighe and Ferrara, 1994). For example, an authentic assessment of a student's ability to write a business letter might include having the student write a letter requesting an interview to gain information on the tasks involved in a specific job. In other words, the task is authentic to daily life; it assesses competencies the student would use in non-classroom settings (work, home, etc.). Typically, authentic assessments require students to coordinate and apply the multiple skills that underlie the effective accomplishment of a task.

Interest in monitoring students' ability to perform "authentic" tasks has led to the development of compatible methods of assessment, or *performance-based assessments* (McTighe and Ferrara, 1994, p. 15). Performance-based assessments often include the use of a *rubric* (p. 15), a guide that specifies the criteria used to judge the acceptability of performance. This type of assessment has been gaining in popularity because it assesses the higher level coordination of abilities that are often splintered in instruction and not recognized with other forms of assessment. The purpose of performance-based assessments is to directly address whether a child can apply learning to tasks he or she needs to perform in daily life.

Matching Assessment to the Type of Learning

Authentic assessment is also associated with the concept of validity—i.e., whether the procedure or tool assesses what it is intended to test (Rhodes & Shanklin, 1993). In this respect, assessment is authentic (valid) when the method appropriately matches the type of learning specified by the goal. For example, an exercise in handwriting, copying letters and words to form letters correctly, is not a valid assessment of a student's ability to put ideas into print (write). In order for assessment to meet the criterion for validity, the *intent* of the instructional goal must be clearly understood, elicited with appropriate instructional activities, and monitored with a corresponding assessment procedure. The approach to assessment should be well suited to the type of learning examined. McTighe and Ferrara (1994), describe approaches available with categories similar to the following:

- paper-and-pencil: selected response items (e.g., multiple choice, matching)

- paper-and-pencil: constructed response items (e.g., fill in the blank, short answer)

- performance: demonstrations of products (e.g., reports, showcase portfolios, presentations)

- performance: demonstrations of process (e.g., read-alouds, anecdotal records, working portfolios, interviews, conferences)

These approaches represent both traditional and alternative methods of assessment. Some are better suited to assessing one kind of learning than they are another. For example, when used appropriately, selected response tests are valid, efficient methods of assessment—quickly, easily, and objectively scored.

These tests are especially effective for assessing certain types of declarative knowledge. They are limited however, as discussed in Chapter 1, in both the amount and kind of information they can obtain. These tests are not as effective as other methods for assessing the application of multiple types of knowledge in "real world" tasks, as described above, nor are they a good choice for evaluating certain types of learning, such as creativity, use of language (conversational or written), or social skills (McTighe & Ferrara, 1994).

The other approaches to assessment (performance assessments and constructed response items) are more effective for examining procedures, processes, affect, and competencies demonstrated through social interaction. They are better suited for assessing how well students carry out authentic tasks. Further, they provide a wider range of ways to find out what children know or can do (print as well as non-print assessments). Since they are open-ended (do not limit responses with selections), they capture more variation and detail about students' learning. One of the drawbacks of this kind of assessment, however, is that it often relies on judgments of criteria that may be time-consuming and difficult to develop. These criteria, too, may be subject to differing interpretations unless they are clearly defined and agreed upon. As with all methods, teachers who use these approaches—whether written or not—must be sure that the assessment does not inadvertently depend upon proficiencies a student does not have.

Matching Method to Purpose: "Checking Up" Or "Finding Out"

A final consideration in the match between the method of assessment and the type of learning is whether they are suited in stance or attitude (Chittenden, 1991, p. 29). Teachers assess for different reasons, including to "check up" or "find out" (Chittenden, 1991). If the intent is to "check up," then the assessment is based on criteria. The learning is assessed according to a standard (right answer, expected or desired behavior, etc.). If, on the other hand, the intent is to "find out," then the assessment is open-ended and used to discover information about a child's learning that is unspecified—not evaluated according to criteria or standards. For example, to "find out" how well a child applies background knowledge to understand written text, "kid watching" (Goodman, 1986), or open-ended observation, works well. If the goal is to "check up" on whether students know the dates of specific historical events, then teachers must use these dates as the criteria against which they judge the students' responses. In this case, multiple choice, matching, or constructed response items may be effective and efficient, but teachers should also consider assessing such knowledge directly through conversation.

In summary, authentic assessment methods are those that:

- assess tasks that students need to use in real life,

- effectively elicit the type of learning to be assessed (and do not inadvertently depend on competencies a student might not have or be expected to have), and

- match the purpose of the assessment—whether the purpose is to gather open-ended information about learning or to assess learning with criteria or standards.

A Broad, Comprehensive Approach to Assessment

Assessing literacy effectively will mean using a variety of methods—a comprehensive approach to assessment. The following framework illustrates the different types of assessment needed in a comprehensive, balanced program (Anthony, Johnson, Mickelson, & Preece, 1991; Johnson, Anthony, Field, Mickelson, Preece, 1988; Routman, 1991):

Observations of Processes (Methods that *describe* conversational or written language processes, responses, and attitudes in use, e.g., interviews, retelling, etc.)	**Observations of Products** (Methods that *describe* learning by examining products of students' efforts, such as portfolios)
Classroom Measurement (Tests and other procedures that are used to *measure* learning according to classroom instruction, e.g., teacher-made tests that are graded)	**Decontextualized Measurement** (Methods that *measure* learning according to criteria not directly associated with instruction, such as standardized tests)

This framework represents the kinds of assessment that should be used in a literacy program. It includes the use of observational assessments (the top two quadrants) as well as methods that measure learning (bottom quadrants). It also demonstrates the distinction between assessment that examines the process of conversational and written language use (top left quadrant) and that which examines the products of learning (top right quadrant).

In the lower quadrants, the distinction falls between methods of measurement that are directly tied to classroom instruction (contextual) and those that are based on other criteria (decontextualized). As mentioned, a comprehensive assessment *program* will include all of these approaches to assessment. However, they are not equally applied when taking into account different purposes for assessment and children with different levels of competency (Johnson et al., 1988).

- For the purposes of planning instruction, observational methods and alternative methods of classroom measurement (represented with the top two and bottom left quadrants) should be relied on more than traditional forms of measurement.

- Observational methods should be especially prominent in the evaluations of younger children and older children whose competencies are at lower levels of development.

- Traditional measurement types of assessment should be used to supplement this information (to confirm observations), their use gradually increasing as children become more competent in their use of language.

Observational methods can provide descriptions of learning that help determine instructional needs. Newer, alternative forms of measurement tend to be more descriptive and thus better suited to this purpose. The more traditional forms of measurement (e.g., scored or graded paper-and-pencil tests with selected response items) provide less information, especially when they are not related to classroom instruction (decontextualized). Also, they are not as effective in assessing higher-level problem solving, or thinking skills, and rarely take into account issues related to second language competency. These methods—traditional measurement—should be gradually incorporated and used to confirm more descriptive assessments.

[It should be noted that in some cases the same tool, or method, may be used either observationally or to measure learning, or to do both. For example, retelling a story—an assessment method described later in this chapter—may be used informally to obtain descriptive information about a student's or group of students' comprehension of a story. It may also be used to obtain a comprehension score for an individual student. At times, it may be used for both purposes—to observe and to measure. In other words, the *use* of some tools, rather than the tool itself, places it in a particular quadrant.]

Observing Processes and Products of Literacy

Observations of the processes and products of literacy should be used extensively as a child is developing competency in conversational and written language. Often teachers use observational assessments with younger, preschool age children and then less and less as children grow older. As mentioned previously, relying solely on traditional assessment that measures learning is not enough to uncover the complexity of deaf children's use of language, both conversational and written.

It is especially important to observe the processes children apply as they use language (conversational and written) in the early stages of learning to read and write. For example, beginning readers are learning to integrate the *cueing systems* (semantic, syntactic, graphophonic, and experiential knowledge) that support reading. As described in Chapter 2, these systems include what students have internalized about the semantics, graphophonics, and syntax of a language. As they begin to read, students learn to apply this knowledge about language (conversational and written), plus their experiential knowledge, to comprehend print.

Through observation a teacher may see patterns emerge in the use of these cue systems that indicate a direction for instruction. One child may overuse graphophonic cues, guessing at unfamiliar words based on the initial letters but not determining if his or her choices make sense in other ways (e.g., using other cueing systems). Another child may be exceptionally good at figuring out unfamiliar words by relying on what he or she knows about the topic (e.g., strength in using background knowledge). Still another child may recognize so few words automatically that he or she is overwhelmed by the reading task. Observational assessment can obtain information about both effective and ineffective strategies that deaf (and hearing) children use in the reading process.

With deaf children, the reading process should be observed to answer three kinds of questions:

1. How well developed is their knowledge of the world and of language (both conversational and written)?

2. How competently do they apply their knowledge about language and the world to the task?

3. What strategies do they use to monitor and support comprehension?

The results may indicate very different directions for the instruction of individual children. For example, if a child's conversational language has not yet developed to the level needed to support reading, writing, and related academic discussion, then this development should be an instructional goal. In other children, their conversational language may be well developed, but it may be a different language (ASL or another spoken language) from the one in print. Their knowledge of the written language may be less developed. In such cases, these children need activities that will facilitate their understanding of the written language system—activities that will increase their knowledge of the words and their understanding of syntax. In other words, they need lots of meaningful exposure to English text.

It is important, also, to give "products" of literacy a broad interpretation for deaf children. "Products" should include examining what children know through all forms of the expression of thought—sign, writing, art, music, dance, etc. In many cases, assessing what children know directly through conversational language may result in a more detailed, accurate assessment of their knowledge. Observational assessments open the possibilities of *what* can be assessed (types of learning) and *how* it can be assessed, often with methods that go beyond paper and pencil.

Measuring Literacy

Criticisms of traditional assessment by measurement have been discussed elsewhere in this text. They are reinforced in *Best Practice: New Standards for Teaching and Learning,* by Zemelman, Daniels, and Hyde (1993). These authors believe that the pressure to justify grades has forced teachers to expend tremendous amounts of time and energy finding ways to "...quantify, measure, score, compute, and record assorted aspects of kids' behaviors" (p. 187). They also believe that the goal of classroom assessment, to guide instruction, has been lost in this effort to "feed the grading machine" (p. 187). Further, these authors claim that the extensive use of measurement has created a competitive educational atmosphere that is harmful to some students.

These criticisms are aimed at the *extensive* use of this type of assessment in the classroom—the widespread practice of recording learning with scores and letter grades. Teachers should not eliminate measurement, but they should redirect its use. A more judicious use will consider the following issues:

▶ *What should be measured (what kinds of learning)?*

▶ *When (at what point in development)?*

▶ *For what purpose?*

▶ *How often?*

▶ *How (what is the best approach to measuring a specific type of learning)?*

By redirecting the use of measurement and putting it into the context of a broad, comprehensive approach to assessment, teachers can more effectively gain the information they need for planning.

One of the ways in which teachers are redirecting measurement is by developing performance-based procedures—a descriptive approach to assessment by measurement. As mentioned earlier and exemplified later in this chapter, performance-based assessments are often scored with rubrics that define the criteria for judging the performance. Further, performance-based methods are often developed to assess how students apply knowledge in real-life tasks, rather than to test skills as discrete entities. In this way, the tests are more authentic.

In summary, classroom assessment should emphasize the use of observational, alternative methods that have the potential to examine both the processes and products of learning. This is especially true for the assessment of young students (preschool-elementary) and older students performing at lower levels of development. As students become older and more proficient, assessment practices may gradually incorporate traditional measurement and decontextualized tests, such as district, state, or other achievement tests. Because of their importance and because they are not as well known, the next section will discuss methods of alternative assessment.

Alternative Methods of Assessing Literacy

Alternative procedures of assessment discussed here include observational methods and classroom methods of measurement that are performance-based. The use of these procedures for providing instructional information is now widely advocated for hearing children; their use with deaf children is no less important for the following reasons:

1. Collectively, alternative procedures have the potential to assess a broader definition of literacy—one that includes different kinds of learning as represented across areas of development (e.g., areas indicated with components in the Stages of Literacy Development; see discussion in Chapter 2 and **Appendix A**).

2. Alternative methods assess learning using multiple approaches. Thus, they have the potential to capture a more comprehensive and accurate picture of

a child's learning than the use of any one method, such as paper-and-pencil tasks, alone.

3. Deaf children often develop competencies in conversational and written language (reading and writing)—in many cases as different languages—over a longer span of time than their hearing peers. A descriptive stance, as indicated with alternative assessment, should be maintained throughout this development to help determine strengths and instructional needs.

4. Alternative assessments, by their descriptive nature, can provide data about progress and place it into a framework that examines the information according to long-term development (e.g., developmental levels indicated with Stages of Literacy Development). In this way, patterns of development emerge that help define long-term instructional goals.

Following in this section are examples of alternative methods for assessing deaf children's progress in literacy in the classroom. These methods, listed below, do not represent the range of alternative assessments available, but include some of the better known procedures:

- Anecdotal records

- Interviews and surveys

- Checklists

- Retelling

- Observations of miscues during reading

- Performance-based assessments and rubrics

- Portfolios

- Hierarchical Rating Scales

The intention here is to provide an overview of these methods. For that reason, the descriptions may not contain enough detail to support using a method for the first time. In these cases, please consult the growing number of publications on alternative assessment for further information. Remember, too, that these examples and other assessments should contribute to triangulated decisions about children's strengths and instructional needs. That is, teachers should base instructional decisions on data gleaned from no fewer than three sources of assessment.

Anecdotal Records

This method records observations of processes or products. It can examine all types of learning represented in all areas of development. Further, anecdotal records can examine learning from an "open-ended" perspective and also be used to "check up," or observe children with specific criteria in mind. Anecdotal records involve taking notes about children either during activities or immediately following them, depending upon which system a teacher finds most effective and convenient. Teachers often keep notebooks in which they can jot down comments about students. During an activity, they might put a mark (e.g., + or –) next to students' names to indicate the nature of their performance in the activity. Later, they can describe these marks according to the criteria they used in the observation. Anecdotal records are more manageable when the observation focuses on certain children and on a specific activity.

Interviews and Surveys

Interviews and surveys assess what children know about themselves (the next chapter, "Involving Others in Assessment," has further discussion on these methods). They are more effective with children who can reflect on their knowledge and competencies—typically, older children. However, their use also promotes reflective thinking by suggesting to children that they examine characteristics of their learning. For that reason, they should be used with all ages. As with anecdotal records, these methods can provide information about a range of types of learning. They can be open-ended ("How would you describe yourself as a writer, and why?") or address a specific area of competency or type of learning. For example, questions about reading habits at home can assess interest in reading. Or, questions such as, "What do you do when you come to a word you don't know?" can assess a student's use of specific strategies.

Checklists

Checklists (created or selected by the teacher) can guide and record observations according to criteria. They, too, can facilitate observations of all types of learning across all areas in the development of literacy. Teachers should tailor checklists to the appropriate level of development for individual children and use them indicate individual strengths and instructional needs.

The Stages of Literacy Development (**Appendix A**), or similar tools, can serve as a basis for developing checklists in two ways: 1) teachers can take items directly from the Stages to create checklists, or 2) they can develop supplemental checklists that provide more detail about specific competencies. Many of the items in the Stages could be described in more detail for a specific level of development. For example, two supplemental checklists were developed for items in the component "text knowledge/comprehension strategies."

- *The Early Reading Checklist*. This checklist provides more detail about observations of emerging and beginning readers.

- *The Reading Checklist*. This checklist provides more detail about students who are reading connected text—late beginning, developing, and maturing readers.

These two checklists are found in **Appendix C.** They provide further information about reading by describing selected items from the Stages in more detail as shown in the example below.

Item from Stages of Literacy Development	Same Item Described in Reading Checklist
• Successfully uses and monitors a variety of strategies for comprehension (e.g., main idea, inferencing, summarizing)	• Understands cause-and-effect relationships • Can identify pronoun referents • Understands figurative language • Can make text-based inferences • Identifies main ideas of a passage or story • Summarizes events in stories • Summarizes main ideas in expository material

Teachers also may select checklists (as opposed to creating them) that will support observations of an *area* in the development of literacy. For example, checklists are provided with the Kendall Conversational Proficiency Levels (P-Levels), to help teachers assess students' *communicative competency*. Teachers use these checklists to determine a child's placement on a developmental scale that describes levels of communicative competency with conversational language. They are not used to assess writing. The checklists, in addition to determining placement on the scale, indicate strengths and needs in competencies that underlie communicative competency. The P-Levels, including the checklists and how to use them, are described in **Appendix B.**

Below is an example of one level on the scale and the accompanying checklist of questions that teachers answer with "yes" or "no."

Conversational Proficiency (Conversational Language) Level 3: The child manages to communicate a lot more than she[6] actually puts into words, but relies less on the immediate physical context than at P-2, since she uses phrases and short sentences. She knows more words than others can keep track of easily. She talks about what she does while doing it and can request lots of different things and services. She can identify many actions and things in pictures and can describe people and objects by their familiar features. She talks about where things are, where they are going, and who owns them. She can use short phrases and sentences.

Accompanying Checklist for Assessment:

Criteria Number	Criteria Questions	Yes	No
3.1	**Does the child refer primarily to things that are of interest to her?** (reference still tied to the immediate environment)		
3.2a	**Does the child communicate about a substantial number of objects and actions affecting her?** (that is, too many to keep track of readily)		
3.2b	**Does the child communicate about the location of objects?**		
3.2c	**Does the child communicate about the destination of objects when they are moving or being moved?**		
3.2d	**Does the child communicate about both temporary as well as more or less permanent characteristics of people and objects?** (e.g., "dirty," "wet," "hot," "cold," "sad," "big")		
3.2e	**Does the child communicate about who owns what and what belongs to whom?**		
3.3	**Does the child link what she says to what others say in any way?** (child may comment on same topic as the preceding adult comment, but this is primarily because they are sharing the same context, or focus of interest. The comment creates text more through the immediate environment than through an actual reference back to the adult's comment)		
3.4a	**Does the child use language to represent a broad range of her actions?**		
3.4b	**Does the child use language to affirm the presence of a substantial number of objects, note (or call for) their absence, disappearance, or removal, and note (or try to bring about) their return?** (e.g., uses language to comment on such things as when she hides an object, someone leaves, she has finished eating something, she has used up her supply of some material; also asking for a return or more of these things)		
3.4c	**Does the child use language to request a broad range of objects and services?** (asks for foods, toys, clothing, help getting dressed, turning on the TV, going on an excursion, etc.)		
3.4d	**Does the child use language to identify objects and actions in pictures?**		
3.5a	**Does the child usually use utterances consisting of at least two syntactically related components?** (e.g., "iron hot," "more cracker," "no bug," "doggie come")		
3.5b	**Does the child provide enough information for others to figure out what she has left unsaid?**		

---

[6] To reduce complexity, each of the P-Levels alternates between male and female gender when referring to a child.

Retelling

Retelling (e.g., Miller, 1995; Rhodes & Shanklin, 1993) is an example of a procedure that uses a checklist to assess a specific task—reading comprehension. The checklist guides teachers' observations of a child retelling a story (or expository text), and is used to determine his or her level of comprehension of that text. When assessing story comprehension, the most frequent use of retelling, the child retells a story in conversational language after reading it; the teacher records the information the child includes by marking the checklist. Retelling examines a student's comprehension as a whole and in a more natural, "real life" context than do more traditional approaches, such as written questions.

The retelling checklist for story comprehension includes either: 1) important information about the specific story, such as lists of the characters and important events in that story, or 2) the *kinds* of story information, based on story structure, that the teacher should look for in the child's retelling. This would include items such as characters, problem, solution, major events, and perhaps theme. Because it is time-consuming to create individual checklists for specific stories, many teachers find it more practical to use a story structure checklist, such as the one provided below (Miller, 1995; Morrow, as cited in Rhodes and Shanklin, 1993).

Retelling Checklist

Title of Story: _____

Student: _____

Directions:
Score 1 point for each item below that the student includes in a retelling.

Story Items	Student Includes:	Score as:
Beginning/Introduction		
Introduces the story in some way (e.g., "This story is about [character] who....")		1
Tells about the main characters		1
Tells about other characters [score = number of other characters told ÷ total number of other characters]		1 (or a percentage of)
Tells about the setting or context (e.g., where things happen and timing, if relevant)		1
Story Problem		
Tells about the main character's problem		1
Events		
Tells important events in the story [score = number of important events told ÷ total number of events]		1 (or a percentage of)
Resolution/Ending		
Tells how the story problem is resolved		1
Tells how the story ends		1
Story Sequence		
Retells the story in logical sequence (e.g., introduces characters, tells about problem and events as they unfold). [Score 2 points for completely correct, 1 for partially correct, 0 for no sequence.]		2, 1, or 0
Student's points (maximum possible score = 10)		

With a "formal" retelling, upon completion, the teacher determines a comprehension score indicating the percentage of information on the checklist that the child correctly included in the retelling. With the example above, the maximum number of points a child could receive is 10. Most items, or elements, must be included in the retelling for a student to receive a point. For example, mentioning or discussing the main characters is essential—these must all be named for the child to receive one point. Two items on this checklist, however, are derived by computing a fraction—the total number of "other" (not main) characters or episodes in the story divided by the number of these that the child mentions.

Informal retelling does not necessarily include scoring the performance—the assessment is used for descriptive purposes alone. For example, the teacher uses the assessment to ascertain which parts of the story the child understood and which parts the he or she might not have understood. Retellings should be used for this purpose—to describe comprehension—even when they are used formally, or to obtain a score. Retelling checklists, such as the example provided here, can also help a teacher monitor a child's understanding of story structure. Children who have an internalized a sense of story parts—setting, problem, solution—often represent this in their retelling if they understand the story. This understanding of structure—acquired by many children from being read to—in turn facilitates comprehension.

Because the assessment of retelling has children explain what they know in conversational language, it eliminates the possibility that competencies in writing, including motor skills, might influence the results. For this reason, retelling is a more valid assessment of comprehension. Also, the procedure allows teachers to probe for more information and clarification. Children also must be familiar with the procedure of retelling a story before a teacher can rely on it to assess their comprehension.

Using retelling with children who converse in ASL requires that the rater have a high level of proficiency in that language in order to obtain a reliable assessment. In many cases, it is advisable to have more than one person evaluate the retelling, including a native user of the child's conversational language. Videotaping the retelling will allow it to be viewed by different people at their convenience.

Observations of Miscues During Reading

Miscues (Goodman & Burke, 1980) are observable differences between what a child reads aloud (with sign or speech) and the printed text. They reveal information about how children apply various language cues during the reading process—cues based on semantic, graphophonic, and syntactic knowledge. In formal, standardized assessments, such as Miscue Analysis (Goodman, 1976) and Running Records (Clay, 1985), teachers record and later analyze a student's miscues when he or she reads aloud a specific text. In some cases, this information is used to measure the student's comprehension level of the text. (Measuring level of comprehension should not be the primary purpose of these assessments, however.)

Formal assessment of miscues is not recommended here for classroom use with deaf children for various reasons, some of which pertain to the unique uses of language by many students, as explained further in this discussion. Also, the procedures are complex and require extensive training for teachers of all students, deaf or hearing. However, teachers of deaf students can, and should, use *informal* observations of miscues to monitor children's reading processes. These observations are especially helpful for obtaining more information about the strategies that beginning and developing readers use. The assessment reveals descriptive information about individuals that can inform instruction. For that reason, basic information about miscue analysis and suggestions for using this procedure with deaf children are described here.

Observations of miscues were originally studied with hearing children and most of the information about this assessment is based on observations of "oral" reading. The assessment is often used with retelling, a more direct assessment of comprehension. During this assessment—with hearing children—the child reads aloud while the teacher listens and follows along with her own copy of the text. The teacher compares what the child reads (says) to the printed text, examining the match between the two. Each time the child reads something different from what is written in the text, the teacher marks this on his or her text to indicate a "miscue." Miscues are recorded with codes to distinguish different types. Examples of different kinds of miscues include substituting of one word for another, omitting a word, mispronouncing a word, making an error and then correcting it, or reversing two words.

Miscues are analyzed to answer the following questions:

▶ Do individual miscues indicate that the child is making sense of the text (e.g., applying cue systems effectively)?

▶ Do miscues as a whole indicate effective or ineffective strategies using language cue systems?

▶ What are the implications for instruction?

Let us look, for example, at the text sentence, "The cow is inside the barn." If a hearing child read "bath" instead of barn in this sentence, he or she evidently did not make sense of the sentence. The child more than likely chose the word based on the initial letters ("ba" is in barn and bath) and either did not monitor comprehension to see if it made sense or did not use other cues to figure out the word, or both. The miscue indicates lack of comprehension, or ineffective strategy use. However, if a child read "stable" for "barn," he or she probably understood the sentence—the word substituted and the word in the text have the same meaning. Although this second child did not, perhaps, use graphophonic cues (letters) to narrow the word choices down to "barn" instead of "stable," the substitution does not indicate lack of comprehension.

After recording miscues and analyzing them individually, the teacher looks for patterns—both effective and ineffective strategies the child might be using. For example, if the child described above made a number of similar, ineffective substitutions or miscues (e.g., read "bath" for "barn," "car" for "cat," "dog" for "dad"), he or she would be demonstrating a pattern of over-relying on graphophonic information while reading, and not balancing this with other cues to comprehend the text. (Also, such miscues show that the child is not monitoring comprehension, because he or she did not correct these miscues). Instruction should focus on guiding this child to monitor comprehension and to use other sources of information (knowledge of the subject, context, syntax, semantics) to balance graphophonic cues.

The study of Miscue Analysis with hearing children is credited to the work of Ken Goodman (1976). However, Carolyn Ewoldt (1981) has used this assessment to examine the reading processes of deaf children who sign. Her work indicates that deaf children use the same cue systems that hearing children do when they read. In fact, children who sign often have a wider choice of cue systems than hearing children because their conversational language differs from the language they read. In other words, they often have information about more than one language system to draw upon. For that reason, interpretation of their "miscues" (differences between what they sign when reading and what is in print) must be based on knowledge of the students' signed language.

When deaf children sign what they read, their signs may closely approximate the English in the text. On the other hand, their signs may also approximate ASL, with different individuals using this language in varying degrees. For those who are making sense of the text, this is likely to indicate an effective strategy—focusing on meaning and actively, effectively processing the text with the support of their conversational language. In these situations, however, teachers cannot use one-to-one comparisons of sign to words in the text to determine these strategies.

The structures of the two languages—conversational ASL and written English—are too different for a one-to-one match to exist and for this to provide information about the use of strategy. In fact, expecting a deaf child who converses in ASL, for example, to sign each word in a text (match signs to text) may distract the child from focusing on the meaning and result in introducing an ineffective strategy for comprehension. Therefore, *observations of miscues should focus on the match between the **meaning** of the text and the **meaning** of what the child signs.* To do so, the observer must be proficient in ASL. Examples of observable strategies (tendencies) include:

Ineffective strategies

- Does not register lack of comprehension; continues to read and does not look puzzled or confused; does not go back and make corrections, does not pause and attempt to work through confusion.

- Does not balance the use of graphophonic information with other cues to make sense of text (sees "-at" and signs "cat" for "hat")

- Uses a form of a sign that does not match the meaning of the text (signs "spring" as in season when text reads, "He *springs* forward to catch the ball.")

- Excessively fingerspells during reading, another demonstration of over-reliance on graphophonic information (fingerspelling may naturally increase with difficulty of material, however—check comprehension to find out if it indicates an ineffective strategy)

- Does not "chunk" meaning in print into meaningful units of sign

- Leaves out information that is critical to understanding

Effective strategies

- Registers dissatisfaction when things don't make sense: rereads, looks puzzled, tries to work through confusion, asks questions

- Signs and print match in meaning, but not necessarily in structure (e.g., sign for "springs forward" resembles "jump;" "point" is used for written pronoun)

- Reads in meaningful units of sign with fluency

- Fingerspells appropriately and not excessively

- Uses ASL for effectiveness and efficiency (e.g., may invent name signs for characters, rather than fingerspelling names each time they appear; may use ASL when it more effectively captures the essence of the text)

In most cases, deaf children, just as hearing children, should read silently so that they can focus more easily on the meaning of the text. However, there are times, as indicated above, when a teacher should examine the reading processes of beginning and developing readers for more information about their use of cue systems, and both effective and ineffective strategies.

For deaf children who converse in English, observations of miscues may be used in much the same way that the assessment is used with hearing children. In these cases, the conversational and written languages the child uses are the same. With deaf children who converse in ASL, however, observations of miscues need to take into consideration the match between the meaning in sign and the meaning in print if students use their conversational language in the process of reading "aloud." Teachers need to be able to recognize how different children who are deaf use their knowledge of language(s) when learning to read and what strategies they apply to the task based on this knowledge. The goal is to recognize how language knowledge and its use either facilitates or impedes the learning process. Observations of miscues, performed informally and flexibly, can facilitate this goal. The assessment requires, however, knowledge of the reading process, of the child's conversational language, and of written English. Further, these assessments should always be coupled with a more direct assessment of comprehension, such as retelling—in other words, miscues should be analyzed in the context of comprehension.

Performance-Based Assessments and Rubrics

As mentioned earlier, rubrics are often developed and used to guide observations of performance-based tasks—those in which children apply, or have applied, what they know to a task. These tasks, or products of learning, may be signed, written, drawn, or acted, depending upon the form of communication that best fits the target of assessment or task. A rubric may be used descriptively or to determine a score for the performance or product, or both. Rubrics are especially effective when teachers develop them jointly with children. This encourages children to reflect on what constitutes acceptable performance of a task. Whether they originate this way or not, children—especially as they become older—should know the features of a rubric that will be used to assess their performance of a task, especially if the performance is graded.

Rubrics include:
1. a description of the learning expected to be demonstrated by a task or a product, including characteristics of an acceptable display of this learning.

They may also include:
2. a numbered scale (e.g., 1-4) describing the learning according to a range of performances or products from least acceptable, or unacceptable, to highest standards, and
3. "anchors," or examples of products representing each point on the scale.

For example, a teacher could develop a rubric to assess stories children create as part of a study of Native Americans at the time of early settlement. The *targets* for the assessment might include:

▶ *Develop a well-structured story*, one that includes a setting, problem, solution, ending, and well-developed characters.

▶ *Include as part of the story information about one tribe of Native American Indians:* where they lived and when, how they lived (type of homes, means of survival), and characteristics of their culture (dress, art).

The product (the story) could be written, but if the teacher wants to focus on students' knowledge of story structure and Native Americans, then it might be best to have students develop and share their stories in sign. How students will share the story should also be specified as a target:

▶ *Share the story with the class in sign.*

The teacher could discuss the targets with the class and involve them in describing the characteristics of the story for the purposes of creating a rubric. They might also create a continuum of descriptions of the task—characteristics of an unacceptable story, an acceptable story, and an outstanding story.

The rubric for this activity might look like this:
        Rubric scale: 1=lowest; 4=highest

1. The information does not represent a story—major story parts are missing, such as setting, main characters, and events that demonstrate a problem and solution. The information about a Native American tribe is either too vague (could apply to any tribe) or incorrect. Presentation is weak—not clearly communicated.

2. Parts of a story are represented, but some important information may be missing; the over-all structure is weak. For example, characters are named, but not described. Some events are included, but do not connect well and may not demonstrate a good beginning, middle, and end (including problem and solution). Some information about a tribe of Native Americans is provided. The information is mostly accurate, but not detailed. Presentation is clear, but lacking in information and detail.

3. Both the story and the information about the tribe of Native Americans are adequate. All of the major parts of a story are included and make sense. The information about the tribe includes all items discussed as part of the target. The information is presented clearly.

4. The story is complete and contains interesting detail about a Native American tribe. For example, characters, setting, and events are well developed, with descriptions that help the audience visualize information about the tribe. The presentation is clear and includes elements that draw the audience into the story. Examples of these elements include dialogue, feelings of characters, or a surprise ending.

Another way that teachers sometimes develop rubrics is by sorting and describing samples of a task. For example, a rubric for writing a story might be developed by taking examples of students' existing written stories. These stories would be sorted into four or five categories according to similarities—the least well-developed stories in one pile, the most well-developed in another pile, and those in-between sorted into two or three different piles on a continuum between the two extremes. The piles would then be analyzed for shared features—what the students have included (or not included) that makes them similar. Next, these shared features are described as points on a rubric continuum. "Anchor" papers—stories that best depict the features of each category—might be selected to represent the different points. The continuum can then be used to assess stories other students write as long as conditions are similar (e.g., students are similar in level of development; context for developing the stories is similar, etc.).

Teachers need to routinely consider how to present any activity or use any assessment tool with signed as well as spoken or written language. For example, students' signed stories could be videotaped and later sorted and described by teachers to develop a rubric—either a continuum or a single description of the standards for an acceptable story structure. Teachers could also involve the students in this task—reviewing the class' stories on videotape and discussing features that constitute acceptable or high performance standards. This approach should not be used to discuss in negative ways performances that do not meet standards.

Popham (1995) explains that performance-based assessments differ from more conventional assessment chiefly in the degree to which the assessment task matches the type of learning you want to evaluate. "Because performance tasks coincide more closely with such domains (type of learning) than do paper-and-pencil tests, more accurate inferences can often be derived about students" (p. 153). The message here is that children's knowledge should be assessed in ways that best enable them to access their learning with authentic tasks. Performance-based tasks and rubrics should be used to clarify the targets of assessment and the appropriate tasks for demonstrating the targets.

Portfolios

Increasingly, educators are using portfolios, individual collections of students' work, to observe children's progress in literacy. Compiled over time, these collections demonstrate *changes* in students' development and evidence of their use of specific skills and strategies. Portfolios can focus on specific areas, such as reading or writing, or encompass a broader definition of literacy by including work that is signed or spoken (video or audiotaped), artistic, or dramatized (videotaped). They may be used as evidence of growth over long periods of time, several years, or during the current year. As an observational tool, portfolios can be an excellent way for teachers and students to examine strengths and instructional needs. Practices in this method are as follows:

- Samples of work are selected to demonstrate evidence of specific kinds of learning or changes in learning (growth); comments about why the samples were chosen—what they demonstrate—usually accompany the work.

- Students, teachers, and sometimes parents, select the samples, either jointly or separately.

- Portfolio reviews take place periodically between teacher and student and include self-assessment, goal review, and selection.

- Portfolios are used to record evidence of learning and to share this information with others, such as parents.

Aside from these common characteristics, developing a portfolio is a highly individualized process for both teachers and their students. There are many options to consider in the way portfolios are structured. The goal of these decisions should be to create portfolios that are both effective and efficient for those who use them. Too often, teachers and students abandon portfolio projects because the assessment becomes overwhelming to keep track of and implement. Careful planning and limiting the scope of these projects to begin with can avoid this. For example, teachers might initially limit portfolio assessment to a certain time period (e.g., 4-6 months), a select number of students (not the entire class), a specific area in the development of literacy (e.g., writing), or any combination of these restraints. The project should be reviewed at a determined time and broader uses of the assessment reconsidered.

In developing portfolios, teachers can refer to the many excellent resources on this subject, including Glazer and Brown (1993), *Portfolios and Beyond: Collaborative Assessment in Reading and Writing*; and Tierney, Carter, and Desai (1991), *Portfolio Assessment in the Reading-Writing Classroom*. These and similar resources provide detailed discussions about the traits listed above and also provide helpful information for establishing portfolios. Pierce and O'Malley (1992) suggest developing portfolio assessment according to the following guidelines:

Designing the portfolio:
What is the scope of the portfolio (reading and writing or a broader definition of literacy)? Does it provide information about progress for the current year or over a longer period of time? What kinds of learning will the portfolio assess? What methods and products will best demonstrate this learning?

Planning for and collecting the necessary data:
Where will the portfolio be kept? What will be used to contain the products? Who will have access, and when? What criteria will be used to select items? Who will be involved in determining the criteria? Will certain items be required and others optional? Who will select items, and when?

Analyzing the portfolio's contents and using the results:
How will students and teachers analyze the contents of the portfolios? How will they set goals? When? What will the procedures be for conferencing with students? How will parents be involved, and when?

The next chapter, "Involving Others in Assessment," also describes portfolio use. As discussed in that context, portfolios provide an excellent way to involve students in reflecting on their own progress. They are also an effective way to involve parents in assessment. Further, portfolios strengthen the relationship between assessment and instruction by systematically reviewing the products of learning and using this information to establish instructional goals.

Hierarchical Rating Scales

This type of measurement uses a continuum of descriptive levels of proficiency to evaluate students' work or performance. An example of a hierarchical rating scale previously mentioned is the P-Levels (**Appendix B**), a rating scale of communicative competency. Checklists (as described earlier) determine placement on this scale.

Another example of a rating scale is the Kendall (KDES) Writing Levels, included in **Appendix D**. This scale was developed to assess writing samples of students at the Kendall Demonstration Elementary School, part of Gallaudet University's Pre-College National Mission Programs. Both the Writing Levels and the P-Levels depend upon the teacher's judgment to assess the level of competency designated with each scale. One important difference between these scales is that the P-Levels assess a child's *level of functioning* (in communicative competency with conversational language), but the Writing Levels were designed to assess individual *samples of writing*. The Writing Levels may be used to make inferences about a child's level of functioning, but inferences should never be based on a single sample of work.

The KDES Writing Levels scale includes descriptions of writing proficiency at different levels of development from least to most proficient. They are based on actual samples of students from preschool through middle school. The levels are numbered and samples of writing that best represent each level known as anchors are provided. On the following page is an example of one of the levels, Level 4 (on a continuum of 1-8).

Level 4		
	Meaning	Message is limited to M-units Context dependent
	Linguistic Features	*Several M-units[4] *Attempts pronouns *Attempts articles *Adjectives
	Conventions of Writing	Conventional spelling predominates (spelling errors do not disrupt meaning) Some successful capitalization Attempts punctuation Spaced as discourse

---

[4] Asterisk indicates most critical feature distinguishing one level from another.

A teacher may use this scale to assess a sample of the child's writing by comparing the features of the sample to the descriptions of each level of the scale. The sample should have all of the corresponding features described in order to be rated at a given level. In some cases, however, a sample will have all of the characteristics of one level and most, but not all, of the characteristics of the next. In these cases, the rating might include both levels (e.g., a child could be rated at levels 4/5). The Writing Levels may be used to infer a child's current level of functioning given that four samples, written during approximately the same time period, are rated and averaged.

While rating scales are another example of observational assessment, they are also an example of methods of assessment by measurement in that they use numbers—points on the scale—to represent learning. The difference in this assessment and traditional measures of learning, however, is that the number represents a description of learning (rather than a score or measure) and communicates information about criteria that are agreed upon among those using the scale. Hierarchical rating scales such as the P-Levels and the Writing Levels—when used program-wide—build consistency among teachers in terms of the criteria used to guide observations of learning in specific areas. The payoff for the students is that their progress is viewed with information that builds over time—beyond the current year.

Using Assessment to Build a Picture of Long-Term Development

As indicated in the corollaries in the beginning of the chapter, assessment of literacy should build on a picture of long-term development. That picture, however, must include the most current, accurate, and comprehensive information possible about the child's learning. All areas in the development of literacy should be evaluated with methods that will effectively access the different kinds of knowledge represented in each. The areas of literacy defined in the previous chapter, according to components of the Stages of Literacy Development, include:

- communicative competence,
- motivation to read and write,
- text knowledge/reading comprehension strategies,
- application of background knowledge to reading,
- knowledge of concepts of print,
- forms of print in writing,

- development in the writing process, and
- social interactions in literacy events.

Collectively, the methods of assessment described in this chapter are capable of assessing these different areas, although they do not represent the range of methods available. They are representative of methods of assessment that can describe the development of literacy for the purposes of informing instruction. However, as mentioned earlier, the use of these methods should vary somewhat according to the age of the child or the level of development of different competencies as indicated below.

Methods of Assessment Appropriate for All Levels of Development:
Anecdotal records of observations (all areas of literacy)
- Checklists:
  teacher-made or -selected that focus observations on different areas or tasks (all areas)
- P-Levels Rating Scale (communicative competency)
- KDES Writing Levels Rating Scale (forms of writing)

Methods of Assessing Emerging Literacy:

Added to those indicated for all levels:
- Early Reading Checklist (text knowledge/comprehension strategies)

Methods of Assessing Beginning Literacy:
Added to those indicated for all levels:
- Early Reading Checklist
- Performance-based assessment with developmentally appropriate tasks (application of knowledge to "real life" tasks, possibly representing multiple areas)
- Observations of miscues during the reading process: late beginning (text knowledge/comprehension strategies)
- Story Retelling: late beginning (text knowledge/comprehension strategies)
- Portfolios (possibly all areas, traditionally used to assess areas directly related to reading and writing)
- Student interviews/surveys (all areas)

Methods of Assessing Developing Literacy: (changes in italics)

Added to those indicated for all levels:

- Reading Checklist (change of form)
- Performance-based assessment with developmentally appropriate tasks
- Observations of miscues during the reading process
- Story retelling/expository retelling
- Student interviews/surveys
- *Beginning use of graded or scored paper-and-pencil assessments (late developing) to supplement observations*

Methods of Assessing Maturing Literacy: (changes in italics)

Added to those indicated for all levels:

- Reading Checklist (as indicated for Maturing readers)
- Performance-based assessment with developmentally appropriate tasks
- Portfolios
- Student interviews/surveys
- *Increased use of scored or graded paper-and-pencil assessments*

Interpreting Classroom Assessment Data Developmentally

As discussed, teachers need a way to interpret classroom assessment information developmentally. The Stages of Literacy Development were created for this purpose—to help interpret assessment information—and also to prompt teachers to examine different areas of development through assessment. For example, *concepts of print* is a component of literacy (e.g., area of learning) indicated in the Stages. Teachers can use portfolio conferences to examine this area of knowledge by: 1) observing concepts that are evident in the samples of work; 2) noting concepts that students understand as they discuss their work; and 3) observing what concepts students understand—but may not apply—in discussions of goals for their work. Teachers can use portfolio conferences as one way to determine how complete and accurate a child's concepts are. After gathering information about these concepts, teachers could then use the Stages to interpret the level of development indicated.

In some cases, the tools of assessment themselves include developmental information that can be interpreted with the Stages. Two examples discussed in this chapter are the P-Levels and the KDES Writing Levels (hierarchical rating scales). These are shown aligned below with the Stages of Literacy Development according to how the levels in each scale appear to represent different stages of development. (With the Writing Levels, this application refers to the use of the scale to assess level of functioning, rather than single samples of work, a distinction discussed earlier.)

Emerging Literacy	Beginning Literacy	Developing Literacy	Maturing Literacy
P-Levels 3-5	P-Levels 5, 6	P-Level 6	P-Levels 6, 7
Writing Levels 1, 2	Writing Levels 3, 4, 5	Writing Levels 6, 7	Writing Level 8

Story retelling also can add to the picture of a child's development determined with the Stages. Teachers can monitor the development of retelling (the sophistication of the task) with information from the different Stages. Also, retelling can be used to indicate a child's approximate independent reading grade level. Teachers can then compare this information to the levels of comprehension indicated for different stages of development by the Stages. (Guidelines for determining independent reading grade levels are included in **Appendix E.**) The levels of reading comprehension that coincide with the different stages of development are as follows:

Emerging	Beginning	Developing	Maturing
	Pre-Primer-Grade 2 Reading Level	Grade 2-4 Reading Level	Grade 2-4 Reading Level

Teachers should determine each child's level of development at the end of the year by analyzing the assessment data. This helps redefine long-term goals. For some children, a review of assessment data will indicate that all areas of learning (e.g., components of the Stages) have progressed uniformly to the same stage of development. When this happens, the level of the child's development is clear and goals are easier to determine. The teacher will then either focus on further development in the present stage or establish long-term goals to move the child into the next level of development. For many other children, however, assessment will indicate they are at one level in some areas and at higher or lower levels in others. In these cases, the level of development is determined by the most prominent level represented. However, certain criteria, especially a child's level of reading comprehension, should weigh heavily in this decision. The level of reading comprehension indicates the degree to which a child integrates learning in a number of areas. For example, a child who reads at a first-grade level is continuing to integrate the tasks of a Beginning Reader. He or she is not ready for the tasks at the Developing level of the Stages. Different stages of development represent tasks of literacy performed with higher levels of materials.

However, deciding a child's level of development is not as important or helpful as determining the patterns in that development. The pattern is what indicates the priorities for instruction. When assessments indicate that certain areas are not as well developed as others, the teacher needs to establish long-term goals for instruction accordingly. For example, children ultimately cannot progress in print-based competencies without the support of these other areas (e.g., motivation, communicative competency, social interactions). For that reason, areas that are less developed must be given instructional priority.

Also, the Stages do not indicate what a child should learn based on his or her age. Information about normal rates of development may be helpful in observing patterns, especially to determine widening gaps between a child's rate of development and what is considered normal. However, the rate of development, other than during the critical early years for learning language, is secondary to the order of the major tasks of the stages and the interdependency of areas within development. *Children cannot learn what they are not developmentally ready to learn.* For that reason, assessment should focus on describing a child's place in the sequence of development—considering all areas contributing to the growth of literacy. It should indicate instructional direction according to that order, not according to what a child should be learning as prescribed by age.

Conclusion

Programs that approach literacy developmentally use assessment proactively. They monitor literacy with a broad definition of the kinds of learning that contribute to progress. They establish goals according to what children need to learn and then closely monitor progress in those goals. They can perhaps be most proactive, however, by setting goals to ensure that children acquire *all* of the competencies at one stage of development that they will need in subsequent stages. This is demonstrated in the programs for deaf children that put their efforts into developing high levels of communicative competency— conversational language—along with appropriate knowledge of literacy concepts before they focus on formal instruction in reading and writing.

The tools and procedures provided here are limited in number and are given only as examples of the variety of assessments available to teachers for assessing literacy in the classroom. The reader is advised, again, to select and design tools and procedures for assessment based on the principles described in Chapter 1. Also, when evaluating the development of deaf children's literacy, readers should consider the appropriateness of any tool for assessment according to the discussions of authentic assessment in this chapter.

Finally, while classroom assessment of literacy informs—or should inform—teachers about learning for instructional purposes, it also informs students. It shows them what we value in their learning, and this is another way we teach them what it means to be literate. With alternative assessment, we provide students with a broader, more descriptive view of literacy than ever before—one that is not limited to performance in reading and writing. This broader view of literacy more effectively informs our instruction; it also serves to motivate students by emphasizing their strengths in addition to their needs.

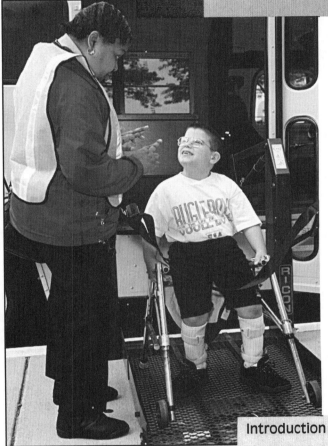

Assessment as a Collaborative Effort: Involving Others

Assessment as a Collaborative Effort:
Involving Others in the Process

Introduction

The previous chapter emphasized using alternative methods to assess literacy. These methods increase an assessment's potential to describe students' strengths and instructional needs throughout development (longitudinally). However, data about students should not come from the teacher alone. Different individuals, contributing other perspectives, should add to the teacher's knowledge of a student, as indicated in the principles of assessment in Chapter 1. The students themselves, peers, parents, and others who work with the students should take part in the process; procedures should be in place to systematize their involvement. However, this concept runs counter to the ways in which others—especially students and parents—are currently involved in assessment. The scenario below illustrates practices that are more familiar.

> Johnny's fourth-grade teacher examines his work, marks all errors in red, and returns it with a score or a grade. Half-way into the grading period, Johnny takes home an "interim report" of his progress. Each subject is marked with "O" (outstanding), "S" (satisfactory), or "N" (needs improvement). At the end of the grading period, Johnny attends an assembly during which the school announces and recognizes the honor roll students. His teacher passes out report cards when the children leave for home that day. Johnny's parents are supposed to sign and return the envelope to indicate that they saw the report. The PTA newsletter that month includes the names of the students on each honor roll.

In other words, students typically receive feedback about what is wrong (errors marked on a paper), the impact of the number of errors (scores or grades on papers), the cumulative effect of scores and grades (interim and final report cards), and whether the grades meet desirable standards or not (honor rolls). Parents obtain information via returned work (if children take it home), report cards, and occasional conferences with the teacher.

These practices are so common we rarely question them. Our society widely assumes that such practices:

1. communicate information to students and parents about the students' progress,
2. motivate students to do their best, and
3. encourage parents to support their children's schoolwork at home.

But do the practices described effectively carry out these purposes? Do they facilitate the goal of assessment in the classroom—to guide instruction? The answers lie, in part, in taking a look at the negative side of these practices:

> Grades on Johnny's work vary throughout the marking period—some A's, some B's, some C's, and even a couple of lower grades. His interim report, however, looks good—mostly O's (indicating an A or B average in the subject). Johnny expects to get on the "All A's and B's Honor Roll" with a little extra work. His parents expect this as well. The day report cards are to go home, Johnny enters the honor roll assembly in a mood of confident expectancy. However, when he is not among those asked to stand and be recognized, he is confused, hurt, and angry. (He finds out later that he got a "C" in math.) What's worse, now he must figure out how to save face among his peers, especially those who made the honor roll. He hides his feelings with difficulty by pretending that he doesn't care. "Who wants to be on the stupid honor roll, anyway?" he clowns as the students exit the auditorium. Later, when he gives his report card to his parents, they are disappointed, angry that he didn't work harder, and baffled by his "don't care" attitude.

> Johnny and other students like him are not the only ones negatively affected by these experiences. During the same reporting period, Matthew, who has been getting all A's, makes a B in physical education (PE). This grade keeps him off the "All A's Honor Roll." He is very upset, and his parents are furious that the school would allow a PE grade to influence his standing for the honor roll. His father meets with

the principal and threatens to take his son out of the school if she does not rectify the situation. ("One of those *pushy* parents," thinks the principal.) Many other students don't make any honor roll, but they aren't surprised—it's common knowledge that they always make bad grades. These students and their peers assume they're not smart enough to do any better, and their parents long ago gave up expecting things to change.

This scenario may seem extreme, but it shows how the practices educators commonly use to involve others in assessment could stand improvement. Current practices like these give the students and their parents little information about the learning process. Also, the feedback given—in the form of grades and scores—comes *after* instruction. Such practices may motivate some students to do their best, but they are usually the students whom the system rewards in the first place—those who tend to achieve acceptable grades. Also, the practices undeniably encourage some parents to support their children's schoolwork at home. However, these parents (and their children) are often competing for best grades and school honors, rather than viewing education as a collaborative endeavor to explore new ideas. And what about the students the system never reinforces? These students receive continuous, negative feedback about their capacity to learn but little information that will support growth and change (e.g., information about their strengths). The same negative, limited information is communicated to their parents.

The practices described are extensions of the traditional, measurement-based approaches to assessment described in Chapter 1. However, the same theories that have led to the development of alternative assessment—the learning theories described in the same chapter—also are leading to new ways of involving others in assessment. They are redefining who should be involved in assessment, why, and how—the subject of this chapter. The outcome of these changes—both in the *ways* and in the *degree* to which others are involved in assessment—is the creation of an *assessment culture* that is different from the one created with traditional practices. Characteristics of these changes in assessment are as follows:

- Teachers assume a reflective role in assessment that includes making judgments based on standards and the contributions of others.

- Students become active, reflective participants in assessing and guiding their own progress.

- Parents become partners in the instructional process.

Reasons Why Others Should Be Involved in Assessment

Changes in assessment indicate that practices should include the students' main teacher(s) and also others who work with the students, classmates, parents and, most important, the students themselves. Involving others in assessment has a dual purpose:

1. Teachers obtain information about the students' development that they cannot observe or access otherwise.

2. Others gain more information about learning, which empowers them to support the process.

Involving Others in Assessment to Learn More About Students

Involving others in assessment enlarges the quantity of data available to the teacher. Information from people in different contexts and with different perspectives enriches the *quality* of the data, also. The main considerations now are *who* should be contributing *what kinds* of data and *how*. Everyone who knows a student is a potential source of new information for the teacher. Special consideration, however, should go to obtaining information from the students themselves, their parents, and others in the educational setting who work with them.

Kinds of data

Data that help teachers know more about their students' literacy development include observations others make about:

- **Competencies students have in different areas of literacy:** communicative competency, motivation, social interactions, text knowledge and comprehension strategy use, background knowledge, forms and concepts of writing, and writing process skills (see discussion, Chapter 2, and Stages of Literacy Development, **Appendix A**).

- **Social interactions that influence development:** *how* others interact with students in language and literacy experiences—what strategies they use; the degree and quality of language and literacy experiences children have outside of school.

- **Cultural values that shape language and literacy development:** language(s) used and preferred in the home, literacy preferences of different cultural groups.

Competencies: Teachers need data from others about the areas of development in the Chapter 2 discussion of Stages of Literacy Development (**Appendix A**). The data should represent different kinds of learning within these areas, as discussed in Chapter 3, including what students know and think, what they can do, and their attitudes and responses to tasks. Teachers can obtain this information from others using open-ended questions as well as tools that address specific areas of development.

Social Interactions: Teachers also need information about social factors that shape development—the interactions, cultural values, and language and literacy experiences that deaf children share with others in different contexts. These factors, especially as experienced in the home, have a powerful influence on a deaf child's progress in ways that may be positive or negative.

Traditionally, education has stressed identifying and compensating for the negative experiences. Teachers need to learn from the positive experiences that children have as well. Information about the literacy experiences of deaf children who have deaf parents is especially valuable in this respect. For example, studies of interactions between these children and their parents during shared reading reveal strategies that deaf parents, conversing in ASL, use effectively to scaffold (Bruner, 1975) their children's understanding of stories written in English—both the content and the language of the text. This information has led to published guidelines others can use when reading stories to deaf children who converse in ASL (Schleper, 1997).

In much the same way that studies reveal information across families, teachers should collect data about individual children and their families. Obtaining this information is part of knowing each student in full, a prerequisite to good teaching as indicated in Chapter 1. For example, several years ago a 12-year-old deaf student enrolled in the Kendall Demonstration Elementary School at Gallaudet University Pre-College National Mission Programs elaborated on the question, "How did you learn to read?" This student, who conversed in ASL, was profoundly deaf and a highly proficient, voracious reader. He explained that, before he could read, he would ask his deaf grandmother to sit beside the television and interpret the captioning for him. As he watched her translate captions into ASL, the television—with the captioning—and her signs were both within his range of vision. Over time, he recognized more and more of the print and depended less and less on the signs. Although instruction surely contributed to this student's education, he associated learning to read with the experiences he had with his grandmother. Undoubtedly these experiences facilitated his literacy development.

Both this example and the study of shared reading strategies indicate ways in which others help young deaf children learn about written language through conversational language—in these cases, ASL— in natural situations. These interactions, and the use of sign language to read aloud or translate written English, play an important role in deaf children's development of literacy. When teachers involve others in assessment, they can learn more about individual children—their strengths and needs—and possibly more about effective strategies to use with all students.

A related consideration that teachers should investigate concerns the degree and quality of literacy interactions that children have with others. Deaf children may be engaged in meaningful, age-appropriate interactions with others on a continuum that ranges from very little to rich and plentiful. The lower end of this continuum may result from the lack of many factors, including:

1. understanding of the child's needs in language,
2. ability to provide the child with appropriate stimulation via language, and
3. understanding of how early experiences and other age-appropriate conditions facilitate the development of literacy.

These factors need to be recognized and addressed by involving others in assessment. The goal should be to improve the amount and quality of children's experiences with literacy as needed.

Cultural Values: Cultural values are another source of information to investigate. These values are intertwined with the language(s) adults use with children and the ways they use language(s)—conversational and written—with children. It is not unusual for a deaf child to experience one language used in the home and a different language or languages used in school. The cultural affiliations and values of the adults with whom they interact influence these experiences. The differences a deaf child experiences may potentially undermine literacy progress.

For example, a preschool deaf child may need and use a visual conversational language in school, but may live in a home where spoken language—English or another spoken language—is used predominantly (with little attempt to learn or use signed language). This child does not have full access to language input or other kinds of information in the home. Conversely, ASL may be another child's first and home language. In this case, if ASL is not used or recognized in the classroom, language and information become inaccessible in the context of the classroom. A third example is when a child experiences different languages, or language systems, used in the school. This child may find information accessible in one classroom but not in another. Inconsistency in the use of language, especially when language use is at odds with the child's sensory needs, impedes learning. Instructional efforts should seek to minimize inconsistencies (between home and school, within school, etc.) and gear language use to the needs of the child.

Cultural values also influence children's choices and preferences in literacy. Children are motivated by the values of those around them—particularly family members. They may reside in homes where conversational discourse, including storytelling or telling jokes, is a frequent form of entertainment. Students may value this social form of literacy over reading as a leisure activity. Or they may value leisure reading, but only in certain forms—newspapers, magazines, and other factual kinds of material—because that is what other people in their home prefer. Students' native values, that is, those based on their home experiences, may complement instruction in the classroom or may be at odds with it. Teachers need to investigate the home values of their students and be open to questioning their own when differences exist. Understanding preferences in literacy—those that originate in the home—is information teachers can capitalize on to motivate their students to learn.

Methods to Use

Many of the same assessment methods discussed in the previous chapter for classroom assessment by teachers can guide or document the observations of others, including:

- anecdotal records

- surveys

- interviews

- checklists

Conferences, a more collaborative variation of interviews, are also an important way to obtain information from others. Regardless of the method, however, the assessment should be sensitive to the participants (e.g., child, parent, other teacher, dormitory counselor), the context of the observation (e.g., home, other classroom, dormitory), and the child's developmental level.

For example, the following questions indicate ways in which developmental differences might influence the kinds of questions asked about an area of development, such as reading. These questions are part of the parent and student surveys about reading (**Appendix F**) designed to accompany the Stages of Literacy Development. Although the questions address similar areas of knowledge (attitudes, interests, behaviors, and strategies), their wording varies depending on the age level of the children involved.

Questions About Reading for Parents of Children at Different Developmental Levels		
Parents of Emerging Readers Level A	**Parents of Beginning Readers Level B**	**Parents of Developing/Maturing Readers Level C**
	What are some things that your child seems to have learned about reading in the last year—ways that he or she has changed?	Same
What are some things you would like for your child to learn about print (reading) this year?	Same	Same
Do you have concerns about reading? If so, please explain.	Same	Same
Does your child like to look at books at home?	Does your child choose to look at books or read at home?	Does your child choose to read things other than homework in his or her free time?
Does anyone read to your child at home or sit and look at books with him or her? Does your child enjoy this?	Does anyone read to your child at home? Does your child enjoy this? Does he or she pay attention to the print during these activities?	Does your child talk about what he or she reads (leisure reading or assigned reading), including feelings and thoughts about the material?
Does your child talk about picture books or pretend to read?	Does your child try to figure out words?	Does your child seem to figure out unfamiliar words—they do not keep him or her from continuing to read or understanding the material?
Does your child notice print around him or her—on labels, in newspapers or magazines, signs, etc. How do you know?	Does your child read simple books independently?	

Questions for parents and others should become a teacher's careful analysis of what he or she wants to know about a student. Simple, straightforward questions—communicated in ways that facilitate comfortable exchanges of information—work best.

In summary, teachers can support their own information about students with data from other different sources. Learning occurs outside the classroom, and the interactions and values of others influence it both positively and negatively. The convergence and divergence of information from multiple sources leads to more reliable, valid decisions about children's progress and their instructional needs.

Informing Others to Empower Them in the Learning Process

Through their involvement in assessment, those invested in the learning process learn more about development and a student's progress. The students themselves, their parents, and others can reach a more collaborative understanding about stages of development, different areas and types of learning within development, and instructional goals. This process builds common ground for discussing growth over time. As a result, others become better able to support instruction in the classroom; they become empowered to facilitate the learning process.

When this happens, the responsibility for a child's learning shifts to include those who influence the process. Traditional assessment, as illustrated in the introductory scenario, places this responsibility exclusively on the teacher, who manages it through his or her instruction and assessments. Students and their parents become the passive recipients of information from assessment via scores and grades, rather than contributors to the process. Further, scores and grades give them only limited information about learning. When others also contribute and receive information via assessment, teachers relinquish some of the exclusive control of learning that has been falsely attributed to them. Assessment more accurately reflects the shared influence that many individuals have on a child's development, and the children become more independent learners.

This change in roles also changes the *attitudes* individuals have about themselves and each other. Parents are less likely to feel left out, helpless, or lacking control over what happens to their children in the educational process; instead, they become team players. Children become more motivated to learn as they come to understand their strengths and help determine their instructional needs. In this process, teachers find themselves less and less in the position of needing to defend or justify their instructional decisions to others.

However, these changes do not occur unless there are procedures in place to define the process of assessment as formally involving others. Effective procedures will systematize and clarify how others contribute throughout the year. The most effective of these examine a child's progress over time. Three examples of assessment procedures that have the potential to perform these functions are:

- Portfolios

- Educational review meetings

- The Primary Language Record (PLR) (Barrs, Ellis, Hester, & Thomas, 1988)

The following sections describe these procedures in turn.

Portfolios

Portfolios were discussed briefly in the previous chapter as a method of assessing students' progress. Although portfolios involve others in assessment— parents, the teacher, peers, others who work with children—they are designed primarily to help students, by students' involvement, and assess their own progress. Through portfolio assessment, students learn to reflect on what they know, what they can do, and what they need to learn. In other words, they become metacognitive—they know more about what they know (Baker & Brown, 1984).

The Importance of Metacognition to the Development of Literacy

The importance of becoming more aware of one's own thought processes—of becoming more metacognitive—has been demonstrated in studies that examine the differences between proficient and less proficient readers. While this topic has been studied extensively with hearing children, some studies examine the effects of metacognition on the reading performance of deaf students (e.g., Baker & Brown, 1984; Garner, 1987, for hearing students; Strassman, Yamashita, as cited in Paul, 1998, for studies of deaf students).

Garner (1987) explains that proficient readers are better at bringing what they know to the task of reading and using this knowledge to help them comprehend. What's more, they do this automatically (Baker & Brown, 1984). However, they are also more *aware* (metacognitive) of conscious strategies they employ to help them read or write. Less proficient readers tend to have less knowledge (including knowledge of strategies), be less competent in using their knowledge, and be less aware of the strategies they do use. (Younger children, by nature of their lesser development, are less metacognitive than older children.)

Proficient readers react differently to different types of text (Garner, 1987). They read passages with familiar structures, concepts, and vocabulary more quickly by applying a great deal of background knowledge to the task. They read more slowly texts that are less familiar—those based on unfamiliar structures and new concepts and vocabulary. They devote more attention in these situations to decoding new words and using strategies to further comprehension—examining headings to figure out main ideas, rereading difficult parts, and using pictures and diagrams. Proficient readers also read more slowly when comprehension breaks down, even when aspects of the text are familiar (Brown, 1984).

Because less proficient readers tend to have less knowledge and not apply what they know as well, they are less flexible in changing approaches depending upon the text (Baker & Brown, 1984; Garner, 1987). Also, they tend not to monitor comprehension the way more proficient readers do (Baker & Brown, 1984; Garner, 1987). For example, they may not be aware when comprehension breaks down (fail to recognize when they "don't get it"). They lack or fail to apply strategies to fix comprehension problems (rarely think, for example, "I'd better reread that last part."). In other words, less proficient readers often do not know when and how to slow down their automatic processing of print in order to debug comprehension problems, yet this is essential to proficient reading (Brown, 1980). To them, reading is more an act of getting information exclusively from print (deciphering each word) than it is an act of using personal knowledge to interpret meaning (Baker & Brown, 1984). For that reason, they tend to seek assistance from others rather than rely on their own resources when they have difficulties (if, indeed, they recognize them).

Studies of metacognition further indicate that self-assessments can be used to reveal strategies to students. They can also serve as a source of instruction in strategies for less proficient readers and writers (Baker & Brown, 1984; Garner, 1987). Through self-assessments, students become aware of the strategies they already use, whether effective or ineffective, and learn to apply new strategies. Therefore, metacognitive (self-) assessment affects literacy in several ways. First, it provides a window through which teachers can observe students' skills; that is, they can see what students know and how they apply this knowledge to the tasks of literacy. Second, it becomes a vehicle for informing students about the efficacy of the strategies they do use reinforcing good ones and pointing out those that are ineffective. Third, it leads to knowledge of more effective strategies—strategies students do not have already—for carrying out the tasks of literacy. Used as a method of instruction, self-assessments can enable students to become more strategic and independent learners. One of the ways in which this may occur is through the use of portfolios.

Metacognition, Portfolios, and Deaf Students

The importance of metacognition and strategic instruction to the development of literacy in deaf students has garnered increasing attention in recent years. Studies in this area indicate that assessment and instruction might address specific difficulties identified for many of these students. For example, Nickerson (1996) indicated that prominent issues in the literacy education of deaf students influenced her study of portfolio self-assessment with college preparatory deaf students. These issues, or areas of developmental need for many students, include:

- developing and using prior knowledge to comprehend written text (p. 51),
- acquiring strategies for determining the meaning of new words from context (p. 52), and
- increasing the repertoire of strategies that can be used to comprehend different kinds of written material (p. 53).

Nickerson translated these issues into goals for her study—areas that she anticipated the use of literacy portfolios would improve through students' self-assessment. In addition to these, which focused on reading, she expected students to improve their writing abilities by learning to assess their written work with holistic scoring procedures (p. 71). In general, she expected students to become more reflective learners as a result of using literacy portfolios with a strong self-assessment component.

The class in her study maintained literacy portfolios for reading and writing throughout the year. The portfolios were used to:

- help students assess their own abilities,
- document what students were learning, and
- encourage the students to become more reflective learners.

The class also conversed in ASL. This enabled students to use their conversational language to talk about what they were learning and their progress in written English. In other words, they could develop a "metalanguage" about learning (ways to discuss their own knowledge) in their first language. Nickerson (1996) indicates that this is another prominent issue in the development of literacy in deaf children that influenced her study—the use of conversational ASL to help students learn to read and write English.

Although this investigation examined portfolio assessment with older students, the procedure can be used for the same purposes with younger deaf students. With younger children, literacy portfolios might include other expressions of knowledge (e.g., videotapes of stories signed, rather than written). In fact, the approaches to the use of portfolios, as well as the contents, should evolve as a reflection of the child's developmental progress. As children become more proficient in reading and writing, portfolios should be used to support learning in this area by focusing on well-defined, important areas of need, such as those described above (using background knowledge to comprehend written text, etc.) However, even with students at higher levels of development, assessment of other types of learning with approaches other than paper-and-pencil tasks can be part of the portfolio. Specific ways to involve students in this procedure are described below.

Involving Students in Portfolios

As we try to help students assess themselves, we should keep in mind two important things:
> 1. *The portfolio process is more important than the portfolio product.*
> 2. *The overriding goal is to develop self-assessment systems.*

(Tierney, Carter, & Desai; 1991, p.109)

Students are involved in portfolio assessments to the degree that they have ownership of the process (Tierney et al., 1991). They should participate in making decisions about the design and development of portfolios, as discussed in the previous chapter, as well as the maintenance and use of these tools. The forms of their involvement include conferences, self-assessments of their learning (the process), and evaluation of products of their learning.

Conferences: Initial conferences between teachers and individual students are especially important for discussing criteria, or standards, for specific assignments and for the portfolio as a whole—i.e., what the portfolio should demonstrate about learning, and how. The teacher should communicate information about the student's strengths and instructional needs and elicit the student's perceptions of these as well. Based on this information, students and teachers collaboratively should establish goals—concrete ways that students agree to work on their own progress. Between conferences, students use this information to reflect on their work, make selections according to criteria and goals, and consider what each portfolio sample demonstrates about learning. In subsequent conferences, students review the contents of their portfolios, reflect on their abilities, determine their progress on goals, and perhaps redefine goals.

Self-Assessments of the Learning Process: Self-assessments initially and throughout the year should reveal information about students' attitudes, knowledge, and strategies used in the process of learning. For example, Nickerson (1996) used a variety of self-assessments to gather baseline information about students as well as to monitor their progress over time. These included interviews, surveys, and questionnaires. With these tools, she examined what students knew and thought about themselves, including how they perceived themselves as readers and writers; their feelings about reading and writing; their habits of study and leisure reading; and their use of strategies before, during, and after reading. The students also used reading logs to record the amount and kind of reading they engaged in outside of class. These assessments informed the teacher and, as previously discussed, educated the students about their development, which encouraged them to become more independent learners.

Self-assessment techniques—whether to use paper-and-pencil or conversational techniques—should be chosen according to the developmental level of the student and purposes of the assessment. In many cases, conversational techniques, such as interviews, may be preferable to paper-and-pencil tasks because they allow students to respond in conversational language and teachers to clarify questions or probe for more information. Nickerson (1996) took notes during interviews she held with students. At the end of each interview she would ask the student to read her notes for confirmation of meaning. Interviews could also be videotaped as a way to record and review progress.

An example of a self-survey questionnaire is provided below. These questions were originally developed as a paper-and-pencil survey of reading to accompany the Stages of Literacy Development model for assessment. However, the author found that the questions were more effectively administered conversationally in informal interviews, especially with Beginning Readers and students who were unaccustomed to reflective questioning.

The original survey included the following questions:

Self-Survey Questionnaire

Is reading hard for you or easy? Why?

What have you learned about reading recently? Try to tell about things you can do now that you couldn't do before.

What do you need to do or learn to be a better reader?

How would you finish this sentence: "Reading makes me feel _____ because_____."

What are your favorite things to read?

Please check the best answer for the items below.	Almost never	Sometimes	Often
When I read, I understand what I am reading.			
When I read, I know most of the words.			
I read at home.			
When I read, I read quickly.			

Specific self-assessments inform the teacher and educate the student. The advantage of these tools is that they can be designed to focus on a variety of areas of development and types of learning. They have the potential to prompt students to reflect on what they know, what they can do, and their feelings about learning. They should be used before, or as part of, initial portfolio conferences and subsequently throughout the year in an ongoing dialogue about progress. Self-assessments are influenced by the degree to which students are able to reflect on their knowledge; this involves learning terminology—developing a metalanguage—as part of these assessments. Students are more likely to develop the ability to think reflectively, and to communicate their thoughts, if self-assessments are conducted routinely and discussed.

Evaluation of Products: Students should be involved in another form of self-assessment—evaluating products of their learning with tools specified for these purposes. In her study, Nickerson (1996) engaged her students in evaluating the content, organization, and grammar of their writing with rating scales for each area. Chapter 3 discusses the Kendall Writing Levels as a rating scale for assessing elementary deaf students' writing (**Appendix D**). Although this scale was designed for teachers, it can serve as a source of information for self-evaluation with students, especially those at higher levels of literacy development (e.g., Developing or Maturing Levels, as indicated with the Stages of Literacy Development, **Appendix A**). As students grow in their knowledge of language and their ability to reflect on this knowledge, they are increasingly able to use checklists that include language concepts and terminology. Children at any level, however, can be taught to reflect on their writing according to appropriately developed criteria.

For example, the Writing Levels contain criteria for judging a sample of writing according to the following features: meaning (the clarity of message), linguistic features (development of language structure), conventions of writing (mechanical features of writing), and story development. This information, based on a child's current level of functioning, can be reworded to serve as a checklist, or rubric, for students to use in evaluating their own writing. Such a checklist should be tailored to the needs of the child and the task. It may not be necessary or desirable to include all of the features from a Writing Level on a student's checklist. The items should be considered goals for the student and discussed in conference. The following is a hypothetical example, minus the features of story structure, based on Level 6 (see complete scale of Writing Levels and how to use them in **Appendix D**):

Writing Level 6 (Teacher's Assessment)	Student Checklist based on Level 6
Meaning: • Message fairly easy to reconstruct—reconstruction problems may be due to context dependency, no sense of audience • Unified topic • Detail	This piece of writing: _____ makes sense _____ is all about the same topic; all parts connect to the main idea _____ tells a lot about what I know about this topic; includes interesting detail
Linguistic Features: • English word order predominates, lack of control of some structures • Attempts a variety of sentence patterns • Uses cohesive elements • May include successful use of verb tense • Successful use of pronouns predominates • Attempts articles • Adjectives • Adverbs	I wrote this in English, the language I read in books. This means I included: _____ sentences. My sentences have two parts: the part that names what I'm talking about and the part that tells something about it. E.g., After she ate, the girl went outside _____ words that connect ideas in my sentences or between my sentences. Examples: and, but, then, because, next _____ pronouns. Examples: I, you, me, he, she, it, they, them, and their _____ articles. Examples: a, an, the _____ adjectives and adverbs, or words that describe
Conventions: • Conventional spelling predominates • Successful capitalization predominates • Attempts punctuation • Spaced as discourse	I checked my paper for: _____ spelling _____ capital letters _____ punctuation _____ how I placed my writing on the page (It reads left to right and top to bottom)

Although the Writing Levels were developed to assess students' stories, they can contribute to rubrics for other forms of writing. For example, if students in one class are learning the proper form for a friendly letter, as a group they can discuss criteria for judging the form. These criteria, then, can be added to individualized checklists that include criteria for the message, language, and conventions of the writing taken from the appropriate level of functioning in the Writing Levels. The following is an example of a rubric for writing a friendly letter that might be used either alone or with criteria from the Writing Levels:

In my letter I included:

_____ **Heading:** my address and the date. These are written on the top right corner of the page.

_____ **Salutation:** a greeting that includes *Dear*, the person's name who will receive the letter, and then a comma. This is written starting at the left margin, two lines below the heading.

_____ **Body:** what I want to say in my letter. This is written in sentences, from left to right, and starts at the left margin, below the salutation.

_____ **Closing:** words I use at the end of my letter. Most people write *Sincerely*, but you can write something like *Your friend*. The closing starts two lines below the body of the letter, to the right of the middle of the paper.

_____ **Signature:** my name. My signature started under the closing.

Students who are maintaining literacy portfolios defined more broadly than reading and writing need appropriate tools for assessing these other types of products. For example, rubrics might be developed for tasks that are signed, rather than written. These tasks should be videotaped so that students can easily review their performance just as they would a written product. Rubrics should be developed before instruction and performance of the task; in this way, they define and clarify the instructional goals for both teachers and students. Even very young children can engage in developing rubrics with teachers for activities relating to literacy. For example, they can assist in discussing which parts of a story should be included in storytelling: characters, what happens (events or problem), and ending.

In summary, students should be involved in portfolio assessment with conferences, specific self-assessments, and evaluations of the products of their learning. The use of these tools should cycle throughout the year in order to demonstrate the ways that learning progresses. These procedures should inform decisions about instructional goals established by the teacher and the student and be used to review progress in these goals.

Involving Parents in Portfolios

Parents also should have a part in portfolio assessment of their children's work. At the beginning of the year, the teacher should explain the portfolio process— the purpose of the assessment, how it is constructed and implemented, and the roles of different individuals in the evaluation process. Parents should understand that portfolios are tools of self-assessment for the students and that all others involved are there to serve that process as supportive facilitators, not critical judges. This information can be communicated in meetings or through letters that are sent home. As the year goes on, parents can be kept abreast of the development of their children's portfolios through newsletters or scheduled conferences.

How parents are to participate in the process—what they are expected to do, how they will do it, and when—should be made very clear. They might:

▶ contribute their own observations about students' progress through surveys, interviews, etc.,

▶ help students keep records of the leisure reading and writing they do at home,

▶ periodically review and discuss with their child selected items from the portfolio in accordance with the student's learning goals, and

▶ review the portfolio's contents as a whole and discuss or write about its strengths, weaknesses, and indications of progress.

The structure of the portfolio process allows parents to participate in an ongoing evaluation of their children's progress through periodic reviews of their work. In addition, it provides information about each child's current level of functioning through the review at the end of the year.

Portfolios educate parents by providing a detailed picture of students' progress supported with specific examples of work. These assessments communicate information to parents about their child's progress—from the student's perspective as well as the teacher's. They also allow parents to communicate their own insights about the child's development to their children and the teachers—insights that may be informed by different standards and different cultural perspectives. Portfolios can work to put students, parents, and teachers "on the same page," and allow them to examine the same things in the same ways.

Involving Other Educational Personnel in Portfolios

Portfolio assessment can be a team effort. The core members of the team include the student, the primary teacher, and the parents. Additional team members might include peers and others who work with students or who know them from school outside the classroom. The design of the portfolio should identify instructional personnel who can contribute to (and should receive information from) the evaluation of the student's progress. Ideally, these portfolio team members would include a cross section of those involved in the educational process in different ways: other teachers, classroom assistants, dormitory instructional assistants, support service personnel, administrators, etc. This cross section should include those who represent the student's culture and share the student's first language (Pierce & O'Malley, 1992).

Instructional staff members of this team need information about the portfolio process. Like the parents, they need to understand the purpose of the assessment, how it is constructed and implemented, and the roles of different individuals in the process. They also need to understand that the primary purpose of the portfolio is self-assessment by the student. Defining exactly *how* the various additional team members will participate is an important step in the design process. They may participate in evaluating selections from the portfolio and contribute their own insights in the culminating evaluation of strengths and weaknesses. Like the parents, they must understand how to perform these evaluations and when. Their input will be especially valuable if they are fluent in the student's conversational language and share his or her culture. One procedure that is useful in involving other instructional personnel in reviewing the portfolio is the educational review meeting.

Educational Review Meetings

Educational review meetings provide a forum for collaborative discussion about individual children among instructional personnel who know them. Programs often use these meetings as needed to discuss difficult issues that teachers are confronting with individual students. However, they should also hold them routinely throughout the year to discuss the progress of all students as a collaborative effort. Educational review meetings can facilitate the exchange of information among all who know students in the instructional environment. Some of these individuals assess students themselves for their own purposes. They may teach a specific area, such as math, physical education, or home economics, or they may be specialists who provide social-emotional, occupational, physical, or academic diagnostic support. Other educational personnel know students from observing them in different contexts and roles. For example, administrators, instructional assistants in the classroom or dormitory, teachers, bus drivers, and cafeteria workers often get to know students in ways that teachers and other specialists do not. Programs should have built-in ways in which all of these individuals can contribute to discussions about the students.

Carroll and Carini (1991) describe the "Descriptive Review Meetings" used at a private school in Vermont as an example of this kind of meeting. They claim that such meetings are designed to "give teachers and other educators the opportunity to gain a deeper, collective understanding of children and development" (p. 41). The goal is not necessarily to come away with fixes for a child who might be having problems, but for all to become attuned to the child's strengths and possibilities as a learner. If a child is having difficulties with learning, concerns should be discussed within this broader context. Procedures for these meetings should be structured and agreed upon. Those used in the Descriptive Review Meetings include (Carroll & Carini, 1991):

- The meeting is chaired by an individual who is responsible for clarifying procedures, facilitating discussion, and making sure that the child's dignity is preserved in the conversation.

- The meeting begins with the primary teacher's *full* description of the child based on information gathered in preparation for the discussion. Features of this description include physical characteristics, moods, relationships, and learning preferences, as well as skills, knowledge, and use of strategies.

- In addition to this description, which the chair summarizes, the teacher presents questions or concerns to the group for discussion.

- Those involved in the meeting share what they know about the student, particularly as it relates to the questions or concerns of the teacher. The purpose of the meeting is for those involved to come away with new insights about the student and directions for future observation and instruction.

These procedures are based on the use of review meetings to focus on the primary teacher's issues of concern, but they also can be modified for routine meetings that aim to balance the input of all involved. Such meetings can be more manageable if they focus on a particular area of development, assessment, or group of students at a time. For example, teams might meet to review students' progress in literacy apart from other areas. They also might meet to reach collaborative decisions about a specific assessment procedure for groups of students, such as P-levels **(Appendix B),** holistic writing scores, or portfolios. In these cases, the kinds of information that should be brought to the meeting need to be clearly specified in advance. The issues, or questions to be addressed, would need to be specified as well. Educational review meetings can serve as part of the portfolio process, and also as part of the Primary Language Record process (Barrs et al., 1988).

The Primary Language Record

In the next chapter, the Primary Language Record[5] (PLR) (Barrs et al., 1988[6]) is examined as a way to keep records on the development of literacy. In this chapter, it is discussed as an example of a system that formally includes others in developing observational assessment information of students' progress. The PLR itself is a four-page form. Teachers fill it out at various times throughout the school year with input from different individuals. The purpose of the process and the form is to create a profile of a student's development over time. The PLR system and form were designed by the authors collaboratively with public school teachers and staff in London, England. Different educational settings in this country use it also. Most notably, collaborations have occurred between London educators and those at sites in California and New York, New York (Cooper, Barr, & McKittrick, 1995). Although the PLR was developed for hearing children, it exemplifies one way that teachers might involve others more effectively when assessing deaf children's literacy.

The PLR incorporates information from parents, the student, others who work with the student, and the primary classroom teacher. It supports other principles of assessment as discussed in Chapter 1 as well. For example, it puts forth a holistic view of the development of literacy, by discussing and recording it as progress in conversational language as well as written language—reading and writing. Also, as an observation-based assessment procedure, the PLR gathers descriptive information about children and uses this to provide direction for instruction. Further, the system is sensitive to language and cultural differences. In gathering information from individuals in different contexts, it prompts teachers to take into account other perspectives on learning. The process of filling out the record, illustrated below chronologically, indicates how different individuals contribute to assessment throughout the year with this procedure.

---

[5] The PLR is discussed here in its original form. The process described and language used in the materials are those developed for public school children in London, England. Readers are urged to examine this system and consider how they could use this, or a similar process, to involve others more effectively in keeping records of deaf children's development in literacy.

[6] Permission to describe and quote from the Primary Language Record is granted by the authors: Barrs, M.; Ellis, L.; Hester, H.; Thomas, A. (1988). *The Primary Language Record Handbook*. Portsmouth, NH: Heinemann Educational Books, Inc.

FALL
Part A: (Page 1)
Records of Discussions:
      A1 child's parents and teacher
      A2 child and teacher
Completed by teacher, parents, child

SPRING
Part B: (Pages 2-3)
Record of Child as Language User:
      B1 talking and listening
      B2 reading
      B3 writing
Completed by teacher with input from all who work with the child

SUMMER
Part C: (Page 4)
      C1 Comments on the record by child's parents
      C2 Record of language/literacy conference with the child
      C3 Information for the receiving teacher
Completed by teacher, parents, child

FALL: **Completion of Part A of the record form by teacher, parents and student**

A1: Record of discussion between child's parents
and class teacher.
A2: Record of language/literacy conference with child.

In the beginning of the school year, the first part of the PLR form (Part A) is completed for each child. In the heading for this part, the teacher must gather information to document the following (in addition to the child's name, age, date, etc.):

- languages understood

- languages spoken

- languages read

- languages written

- physical characteristics that impact the development of literacy

- names of staff involved in development of the child's literacy
  (pp. 10, 11)

Below the heading, Part A is divided into the two sections (A1 and A2) as previously indicated, with space to document notes from separate conferences with the parents and the child. These sections are titled:

A1 Record of discussion between child's parent(s) and class teacher and
A2 Record of language/literacy conference with child (pp. 12-15)

Parent Conference: The teacher confers with the parents to obtain information about the child's progress and capabilities in conversational language, reading, and writing. The accompanying *Handbook for Teachers*—a guide to using the PLR—provides suggestions for conducting these conferences, including the kinds of questions to ask. The *Handbook* prompts teachers to consider such issues as (pp. 12, 13):

1. using interpreters for parents who speak another language,
2. holding the meeting at a mutually convenient time,
3. considering seating that will not put parents at a disadvantage, and
4. deciding who should take notes and how (Should the teacher take notes? Directly on the form? In English?).

It also advises teachers to discuss how the school uses bilingual children's first language to help them learn English.

Student Conference: This conference is similar in many ways to the parent conference. The *Handbook* suggests that this be part of an *ongoing dialogue* that teachers have with their students about their development. Also, the *Handbook* recommends that this discussion be held, if at all possible, with native speakers of the child's language. The conversation should address the child's thoughts about himself or herself as a language user, both conversational and written. Teachers should facilitate these conversations with open-ended questions but expect students to take the lead once they become comfortable with the format and purpose of these talks (pp. 14, 15).

Part A encourages two-way communication between the home and the school at the start of the year. This part also formalizes a way for teachers to obtain information about students that is not accessible through classroom observation. Further, by obtaining this information at the beginning of the year, the teacher can use it as part of the instructional process and address it throughout the year. It starts the dialogue about the learning process—one that teachers, students, and parents should have routinely—in a way that establishes an instructional partnership.

SPRING: Completion of Part B of the record form by the teacher, including information from all who work with the child

The Child as Language User (One or More Languages)

Parts	B2,
B1,	B3

      B1 Talking and Listening
      B2 Reading
      B3 Writing

This part of the form, once completed, will contain input from all who work with the child. Although the main teacher completes Part B, each person who contributes information will sign the form. This part is divided into three sections (B1, B2, B3) on the two inside pages of the form with space to respond to the following directions and questions (shown verbatim):

B1 Talking and Listening

Please comment on the child's development and use of spoken language in different social and curriculum contexts, in English and/or other community languages; evidence of talk [or sign] for learning and thinking; range and variety of talk [or sign] for particular purposes; experience and confidence in talking [or signing] and listening with different people in different settings.

    ▶   *What experiences and teaching have helped/would help development in this area? Record outcomes of any discussion with head teacher, other staff, or parent(s) (p. 19, 20).*

B2 Reading

Please comment on the child's progress and development as a reader in English and/or other community languages; the stage at which the child is operating (a developmental scale is provided in the *Handbook* and referenced in this section of the PLR); the range, quantity, and variety of reading in all areas of the curriculum; the child's pleasure and involvement in story and reading, alone or with others; the range of strategies used when reading and the child's ability to reflect critically on what is read.

> ▶ *What experiences and teaching have helped/would help development in this area? Record outcomes of any discussion with head teacher, other staff, or parent(s) (p. 22).*

B3 Writing

Please comment on the child's progress and development as a writer in English and/or other community languages; the degree of confidence and independence as a writer; the range, quantity, and variety of writing in all areas of the curriculum; the child's pleasure and involvement in writing both narrative and non-narrative, alone and in collaboration with others; the influence of reading on the child's writing; growing understanding of written language, its conventions, and spelling.

> ▶ *What experiences and teaching have helped/would help development in this area? Record outcomes of any discussion with head teacher, other staff, or parent(s) (p. 29).*

This part of the form formalizes the input of others in describing the child's language and development of literacy. It also facilitates the other purpose for involving different individuals—informing them about development in ways that enhance the program's consistency. The information in the directions and in the accompanying parts of the *Handbook* is consistent with many of the concepts expressed in other chapters of this text. For example, the directions encourage those involved to examine a variety of types of learning, including language used for different purposes, attitudes (enjoyment), and strategies. Confidence and independence as a language user are also indicated. Concepts about literacy are exemplified even in the layout of this part of the form. For example, this part was deliberately placed on the facing, two-page spread inside the form to reinforce the interdependency of conversational language and written language (reading and writing) in development (p. 16).

The *Handbook* guides others to consider the first language for bilingual students as well as other languages the student uses or is learning. It suggests that native users of the student's language who know the student should assist in filling out this part. The importance of assessing conversational language use in different contexts, as discussed in Chapter 2, is also reinforced. Those involved in the assessment are directed to consider *both the social and curriculum dimensions of language use* when observing students in different contexts (p. 17).

The directions prompt those involved to assess reading according to stages of development (p. 26). In this way, it encourages the longitudinal view of development suggested in Chapter 2 that is essential for understanding a student's progress for the purpose of long-term planning. Teachers also must consider the effects of reading on writing. This is consistent with Krashen's (1992) theory, also mentioned in Chapter 2, that students acquire much of what they learn about writing primarily through reading.

An interesting discussion in the *Handbook* about writing relates to Paul's (1998) concept of guiding deaf students to develop literate thought apart from reading and writing. The *Handbook* makes a distinction between composition and transcription (Barrs et al., 1988). Composition is described as the actual creation of text, transcription as the act of writing down the text (p. 30). "Text" here refers to stories that are thought out but not necessarily written down. The *Handbook* suggests that teachers help students who are not developmentally ready to transcribe (write) their texts to record their stories in other ways. These suggestions include shared or collaborative writing activities and the use of word processing computer programs. Deaf children can use videotapes to capture texts that are signed.

In summary, completing Part B of the PLR fulfills the dual purpose of involving others in assessment. It helps teachers learn more about their students by including others who work with the students. It also conveys information to all involved about many concepts and principles of assessing literacy. In addition to those mentioned in the previous paragraphs, the concept that learning does not happen exclusively as a function of instruction is reinforced in this part of the form. In other words, all involved are prompted to consider the *experiences*, in addition to instruction, that may be or could be facilitating a child's literacy development. Educational review meetings, as discussed previously, might be used as a way to gather information for completing this part.

SUMMER: Completion of Part C of the form by the teacher, the child, and the parent(s)

C 1: Comments on the Record by the Child's Parent(s)
C 2: Record of Language/Literacy Conference with the Child
C 3: Information for Receiving Teacher

Part
C

Section C1, on the back of the form, provides space for parents to "contribute their own feelings and judgments about the child's work and progress over the year" (p. 35) and to comment on Part B of the Record after it has been completed. The next section, C2, provides another opportunity to formally document the student's thoughts and observations about his or her own progress at the end of the school year. Section C3 provides space for those currently working with the student to update information from Part B if there are changes or additional progress that should be noted. This last section (C3) also provides space for teachers to summarize their understanding of the student's development and needs for the next year's teacher. The directions for this last section include:

C 3 Information for Receiving Teacher

This section is to ensure that information for the receiving teacher is as up-to-date as possible. Please comment on changes and development in any aspect of the child's language since Part B was completed.

▶ *What experiences and teaching have helped/would help development? Record outcomes of any discussion with head teacher, other staff, or parent(s) (p. 35).*

The completed PLR, at the end of Part C, is signed and dated by parents, the class teacher, and the head teacher. The record becomes a permanent profile of the child's progress throughout the year and a part of his or her longitudinal record file.

The strength of the Primary Language Record has been described throughout: It documents development over time, it supports views of development based on theories about learning and literacy consistent with those presented in this text, and it relates assessment information to instruction. Further, it is an excellent example of a procedure that involves others in assessment. The PLR formalizes the roles of others in assessment by gathering information from multiple sources that teachers need to make decisions about students' progress and instructional needs.

Conclusion

The purpose of this chapter has been to emphasize the importance of involving others in assessment. One of the reasons for doing so is to increase the amount and quality of data available to teachers for triangulating instructional decisions. Triangulation was first mentioned in Chapter 1 in connection with the principles for guiding assessment. The term refers to the practice of using multiple assessments and sources of information to make judgments about students' development in literacy. As described in this chapter, the sources of assessment data should include the classroom teacher and the students themselves, their parents, and other educational personnel. Triangulation of this data leads to more valid decisions about students' strengths and instructional needs.

A second reason for involving others in assessment is to change current practices that reflect the false assumption that the classroom teacher is primarily responsible for the learning process. Until practices reflect the importance of empowering others who influence this process, it is doubtful that assessment can effectively guide and improve instruction. It is up to teachers and those who design educational programs for children to structure ways for this to happen— ways for others to be involved in assessment. As described in this chapter, portfolios, educational review meetings, and the Primary Language Record are examples of procedures that can accomplish this goal.

Chapter 5

Record Keeping

Characteristics of an Effective Record-Keeping System

Tools For Record Keeping: Collecting Data at Different Levels

The Assessment Process

Conclusion

Record Keeping

Teachers' professional knowledge and their effectiveness are enhanced by careful observation and regular record keeping.

(Barrs, Ellis, Hester, & Thomas, 1988, preface)

In order to record and analyze assessment data, there are a number of points to consider. First, you need some tools for recording data. Second, it's important that you find the time to conduct assessment. Third, you need to decide ways to record and analyze assessment data that best suit your requirements and needs. Finally, it helps to consider specific techniques that will make assessment manageable.

(Rhodes & Shanklin, 1993, p. 24)

The previous chapters suggest that the classroom teacher gather the following kinds of information about each student:

▶ patterns of growth according to broad stages of the development of literacy, including strengths and weaknesses in the different components (Chapter 2);

▶ data about progress in these components from assessment of short-term instructional objectives—day to day, week to week, month to month—using a variety of types of assessment but relying heavily on *descriptive* assessments or alternatives to measurement (Chapter 3); and

▶ input from the students themselves, parents, and other professional staff members who work with the students (Chapter 4); in this way, others share the responsibility of assessment.

The overriding reason for collecting this information, as discussed in Chapter 1, is so the current teacher can know each student's strengths and needs in ways that maximize effective instruction. Ultimately, then, the purpose of all assessment data is for making decisions about progress in literacy and determining instructional needs. In order to carry out these purposes, the data must be documented and organized systematically. Also, it must be organized in different ways, depending upon who is contributing and using the information. Rhodes and Shanklin (1993) claim that "the key to effective assessment is to use several ways of collecting data"(p. 31). The purpose of this chapter is to discuss ways of collecting, documenting, and organizing assessment data to facilitate instruction—the record keeping process.

As a caveat to the ensuing discussion, the reader is advised to aim for understanding the organizational framework of record keeping, rather than to focus on individual techniques and procedures. There are two reasons for this suggestion:

1. A sense of the overall organization will enable one to see which parts of an existing system are already in place and which need to be added or changed.

2. The design goal for record keeping should be to ultimately have in place a well-developed system at many levels in a program; this should be developed collaboratively, over time, with sustained focus on the organizational framework.

In other words, record keeping is the responsibility of the entire program—not individual teachers working in isolation.

Characteristics of an Effective Record Keeping System

An effective record-keeping system—one that supports the assessment-instruction link—should have certain traits. Essentially, it should reflect the same principles of assessment described in Chapter 1—the same theories (e.g., developmental, holistic) used to support instruction and assessment. In fact, a well-planned record-keeping system should guide those who are using assessment to view development according to these theories. In keeping with these theories, it should indicate that assessment is a shared responsibility, as discussed in the previous chapter.

An effective record keeping system will have *tools* for documenting progress. While recording progress is inherent in some procedures, in other cases this step must be added. Assessment by portfolio, for example, is a system of assessment that documents a student's progress in literacy with examples of the student's work. Maintaining records of work is part of the process. Informal observations, on the other hand, may go unrecorded if they are not documented with anecdotal notes, a checklist, or some other tool. This often has been the case with observational assessment. That is, teachers know a great deal about their students from observing them in the classroom, but this information often is not documented systematically. Records of students' progress need to include this kind of information—data from teachers' observations—in addition to other types of assessment data.

Effective systems must also establish how record-keeping tools are to be used. For example, it is possible to have techniques and tools for documenting classroom assessment—anecdotal notes, test scores, samples of students' work—but not have a system for evaluating the data and using this information to plan instruction. Thus, record keeping must include a clearly defined *process* for documenting, sorting, selecting, and synthesizing data over time. Further, the process must be efficient as well as effective for those involved.

Consequently, there are two issues to address in designing an effective record-keeping system. One involves defining or developing the *tools* for record keeping—the actual means by which one can record assessment data. These tools should satisfy record-keeping needs at different levels of the instructional system: the student level, the classroom or teacher level, and the program level. The other component of design involves making decisions about the *process* of record keeping—the timing and procedures for collecting, sorting, evaluating, and sharing information. This chapter describes both aspects of record keeping—the tools and the process. It begins with a discussion of the tools, and then illustrates the process with an example of how assessment might occur throughout an academic year.

Tools for Record Keeping: Collecting Data at Different Levels

As mentioned above, the tools for record keeping should satisfy the needs of all levels of the instructional system (student, teacher, and program). The system must work to involve students, parents, and other staff; organize information so that teachers understand individual development and instructional needs; and document development in ways that inform others of progress. The system also must put this information into a framework that provides a picture of ongoing development over time—beyond the current year. Examples of tools described in this chapter for these different purposes at different levels include:

Student Level	Teacher Level	Program Level
• Student files • Portfolios	• Records of observations and samples of reading and writing • Teacher files for the class	• Student profiles • Literacy notebooks (Rhodes & Shanklin, 1993)

Record keeping at each level serves different purposes, depending upon who is using the information. Accordingly, it should be controlled by different individuals. Record keeping at the student level, for example, should involve students in assessment. For that reason, the students themselves should become as independent as possible in maintaining these records. Teachers need to be in control of the records they keep at the teacher level. Systems at this level must be effective and efficient for day-to-day instruction and tailored to individual teachers' needs. At the program level, the system supports multiple purposes and should be planned—and used—collaboratively. For example, in addition to supporting classroom instruction, records at the program level are often used to evaluate a program's effectiveness or as a resource for specialists who work with individual students. Records at this level should communicate progress across years in ways that are consistent from year to year.

Further, the contents and use of students' records varies according to developmental level and the purpose of the information. As discussed in Chapter 3, the younger the student, or the less developed the student's skills in literacy, the greater the need for descriptive, observational data to predominate in assessment collections. The answer to the question, *"What is important to know about this student?"* should determine the kinds of information to be collected and recorded. The reader should keep in mind this individual variation in record keeping—according to the level of the students—when considering the examples for each level below.

Record Keeping at the Student Level

Students maintain records of their work as part of becoming involved in their own assessment. The reasons for this—for involving students and others in assessment—were discussed in Chapter 4. Maintaining records enables students to monitor their own progress and determine their own perspectives on their strengths and weaknesses. It empowers them to take charge of their learning— to become independent learners. Teachers facilitate the development of record keeping at this level, deciding together with the students why information will be collected and how it will be used, collected, and stored. As much as possible, however, students should maintain their own records of their work independently. Student files and portfolios are two examples of the kinds of records they might keep.

Student files: Students store their work—both completed products and works in progress—and other items that indicate progress and interests in files or other suitable receptacles in the classroom. These are *working files;* students access them daily, and they are an integral part of instruction. They contain the most extensive collections of data on literacy and demonstrate day-to-day progress. Students date all of the work in the files to preserve a record of their development over time.

These files also serve as a source of materials for the portfolios. Periodically, the students, with the teacher, review the files, selecting items for portfolios and taking out others to be sent home. As with portfolios, the type of work that goes into the file folders needs to be defined. Students might maintain broadly defined literacy folders (containing examples of work and interests in all expressions of literacy), reading folders, writing folders, or reading-writing folders. They also might maintain folders of literate work in other areas of the curriculum.

Files can be organized in a way that represent work that is conversational (e.g., videotapes of signed work or spoken presentations), written (e.g., drafts of stories or written reports), and read (e.g., lists of materials read according to genre). In this way, they would support a holistic view of the development of literacy and encourage students to consider indications of literacy beyond written work. These files might also include artistic and dramatic expressions of literacy. Deciding the possible contents of literacy folders or files—what constitutes examples of literacy work and interests—should be a collaborative effort involving the students. The contents will also determine the type of receptacle needed for the file; in many cases, students will need a larger container than a traditional paper file folder.

Examples of Student Literacy File Contents[7]

- videotapes of learning (signed or spoken) expressed conversationally: collaborative projects conducted with other students, conferences with teachers, stories and reports, retelling of books read, discussions of

---

[7] Contents will vary according to development, interests, and literacy activities.

academic topics from all subject areas, including literacy (stories, authors, etc.),

- videotapes or photos of learning expressed dramatically or artistically (e.g., plays, paintings, etc.), and

- paper-and-pencil expressions of learning: written work in progress and completed; peer reviews of work; journal selections (literature, dialogue, learning log, etc.); self-surveys (interests, strategies, etc.); lists of literacy interests: favorite topics, favorite authors, favorite books, favorite genres.

Portfolios: Previous chapters have discussed portfolios as an assessment method (Chapter 3) and as a process that effectively involves others (Chapter 4). Portfolios also are an important part of the record-keeping system at the student level—a part of the system that is developed with the support of the student files described above. Students periodically review these files for the purposes of examining progress and making selections for portfolios that will give evidence of progress. For that reason, portfolios might be designed to reflect the organization of the day-to-day files—to focus on the same types of learning. What's more, the student with the teacher as a facilitator should maintain them. As indicated in previous discussions, guidelines for the contents could be developed as a class effort, but within this framework, the actual contents of each portfolio should be a matter of students' personal decisions.

Although portfolios will show finished work (completed products), they also should contain demonstrations of work in progress. In this way, they keep records of learning *over time* to show changes. They become *working* portfolios and not merely showcase portfolios. For example, students' stories, including all drafts, might be recorded at the beginning, middle, and end of the year to show changes.

Most often, the optimum length of time for individual portfolio collections is one academic year, although some programs maintain students' portfolios over longer periods. The value of one-year, or current-year, portfolios derives from their intended use—involving students in examining their own development. In this scenario, students individualize their portfolios, and the portfolios include rich evidence of the students' progress and serve as an integral part of instruction. If portfolios are organized at the program level (across a number of years), they tend to become too standardized and limit the amount of detail recorded for any one year. When this happens, they are no longer the student-centered, student-controlled, and student-maintained assessment tool they are intended to be.

Examples of Portfolio Contents[8]

- goals developed in conference with teacher,

- self-surveys, attitude surveys (paper-and-pencil or videotapes of interview/conferences),

- examples of work chosen from files that indicate knowledge, interests, and growth (e.g., work that demonstrates learning expressed in conversation, reading and writing, drama, art, etc.),

- written notes or videotaped conversations that describe reflections about work; what the selections indicate to the student about his or her learning, knowledge, and interests, and

- reviews of portfolio contents by others on the portfolio team (peers, parents, others who work with the student).

Record Keeping at the Teacher Level

There are two considerations for record keeping at this level: 1) how teachers will record data from their own assessments, and 2) how they will maintain records that include both their data and information from others (e.g., students' self-assessments, input from parents). The methods a teacher uses should enhance understanding of the student—indicate strengths, instructional needs, and the effects of instruction. Therefore, record keeping at this level should be integrated with instruction, routine, and easy to use. Individual teachers should determine the procedures according to what they need to know and their own style of managing the data. What they collect, how, and when will depend on the kinds of students they teach, their instructional activities, and their personal preferences for informative, efficient record-keeping techniques. In other words, teachers control record keeping at this level.

As described in Chapter 3, alternative methods of assessment should contribute the major portion of assessment information. Because these are primarily descriptive and observational, it is important that teachers develop a system that is capable of recording this information effectively and efficiently, especially observational information obtained during process activities (e.g., story retelling, discussions, etc.). Often, observations of the products of learning (completed assignments, either written or communicated conversationally and captured on videotape) can be evaluated at other times. Evaluations of students' performances during activities—if not videotaped—need to be recorded on the spot or immediately after an activity.

---

[8] Contents will vary according to development, interests, and literacy activities.

During or immediately after an activity, teachers might use a checklist or keep a pad of loose paper on which they can record notes for all or some students. The system they use, however, should enable them to transfer the information easily to records for each student. For example, they might carry a page of gummed labels on a clipboard in class so they can take notes they can later peel off and add to their files for individual students. Also, they might use note pads to record information; later, separate sheets for individual students can be torn off and transferred to student files. Photocopies of class checklists can be added to individual files.

In summary, teachers need to record information about students continuously. They also need to store this information with other data they collect in ways that enable them to make valid decisions about instructional needs. Two methods that teachers might consider for these different purposes are described in the following sections. The first is taken from the Primary Language Record (PLR) (Barrs et al., 1988) and serves as an example of record keeping of observational assessment. The second is a discussion of teachers' assessment files for the students in their class.

Recording Observations and Samples of Reading and Writing

Throughout this text, the PLR serves as an example of a well-developed assessment system that is consistent with many of the principles described in Chapter 1. The previous chapter describes and discusses the PLR, and this chapter will mention it again later as an example of student profiles. Here, the discussion focuses on the part of the PLR that exemplifies how teachers might record observational information. A form for recording observational information and samples of students' work is an optional part of the PLR.

This Observations and Samples[9] form (Barrs et al., 1988, p. 36)[10] includes four pages for recording observational information, as illustrated below. Each of these pages is described in turn.

---

[9] The headings and directions on the PLR forms, in this and the previous chapter, are given verbatim. Educators of deaf children should focus on the meaning of the information—the wording, in places, might not apply for certain programs.

[10] Permission to describe and quote from the Primary Language Record is granted by the authors: Barrs, M.; Ellis, L.; Hester, H.; Thomas, A. (1988) *The Primary Language Record Handbook*. Portsmouth, NH: Heinemann Educational Books, Inc.

Primary Language Record Observations and Samples Form

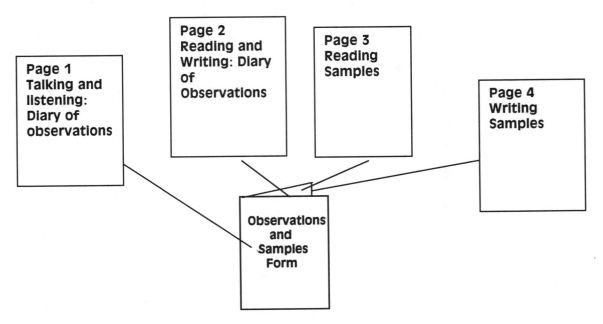

Page 1: Talking and listening: diary of observations (p. 37)

Space on this page of the form is provided for noting examples of a child's use of conversational language. Teachers are asked to consider the following:

- different languages used,

- different kinds of talk (planning events, telling a story, reporting on results of an investigation, etc.), and

- "Experience and confidence in handling social dimensions of talk" (initiating conversation, listening to others' contributions, etc.).

A matrix of social contexts (p. 38) is provided at the top of this page of the PLR for cross-referencing observations with the contexts in which they occur. When a teacher makes a note about the use of language and dates the note, he or she can also enter the date in the matrix to indicate the context of the sample. In this way, teachers can monitor the variety of contexts they are observing. The matrix is as follows (p. 38):

Learning contexts	Social Contexts			
	Pair	Small Group	Child/ Adult	Child with Group/Adult
Collaborative reading/writing activities				
Play, dramatic play, drama, & storytelling				
Environmental studies & historical research				
Math & science investigations				
Design, construction, craft, & art projects				

This matrix supports the concept that proficiency in conversational language needs to be monitored in a variety of contexts, as described in Chapter 2. Conversation is one of the ways in which children learn in all areas and should be monitored as such.

Page 2: Reading and writing: diary of observations (reading and writing in English and other community languages) (pp. 37-44)

This page, like the first, is for recording observations over time of a child's reading and writing in a variety of contexts. The page has two sections, one with space for comments about reading and the other for comments about writing. The teacher records and dates observations for both, including "wider experiences of story" (p. 40) for reading and stories dictated by the child for writing. The guidelines for considering "wider experiences of story" include examination of the following items related to experiences with books and other forms of print: choices and preferences, responses, ability to sustain attention, independence, social interactions (discussions), experiences of "story" (understanding of conventions, demonstrated in story telling, retelling, drama, etc.), critical and reflective thinking. There are similar guidelines for writing, including the child's understanding of written language conventions and the spelling system.

Page 3: Reading samples (reading in English and other community languages); to include reading aloud and reading silently (pp. 45-49)

This page documents information about a child's reading in one setting with a specific text—a "sample of development" (p. 45). The child is asked to read a book, excerpt, or other form of written text, by first examining it and perhaps reading it silently, then reading it aloud. After the reading, the teacher discusses the text with the child. Prompts for recording information are listed on the left side of this page of the form. Teachers respond to each prompt—write their comments—in the space provided to the right of this column. The prompts (p. 48) are listed below in boldface; elaboration is taken from discussion in the PLR *Handbook*:

1. **Title or book/text (fiction or information)**
   - Indicates that assessments should not be limited to fiction or stories.
2. **Known/unknown text**
   - Indicates that either type of text may be used; younger children/less proficient readers may feel more comfortable with familiar material, but this should be noted.
3. **Sampling procedure used**

   - Prompts teachers to document the procedures they use (informal observation, observations of miscues, etc.).
4. **Overall impression of the child's reading**

   - Suggests teachers examine confidence, degree of independence, involvement with text/book (attention, personal responses), and the way the text was read aloud (use of another language, comfort, fluency, pace).

5. **Strategies the child used when reading aloud**

   - Prompts teachers to observe all children for their use of background knowledge in the task.

   - Suggests observing younger, less proficient readers (i.e., Beginning, early Developing Levels in the Stages of Literacy Development, **Appendix A**) for use of book language, "playing" at reading, use of pictures, and knowledge of conventions of print.
   - Suggests that more proficient, experienced readers (i.e., late Developing and Maturing Levels in the Stages of Literacy Development) be observed for use of language cues (grapho-phonic, syntactic, semantic), the balance of use of these cues, predicting, and self-correcting.
6. **Child's response to the book/text**

- Indicates that two kinds of responses should be considered: personal and critical (comprehension, evaluation, interpretation of wider meaning).

The *Handbook* suggests filling out this page once a term (twice a year) or photocopying it to be used more frequently (p. 45). It also recommends that teachers use informal observations, running records, and miscue analysis as procedures for obtaining information (p. 45). The author suggests using observations of miscues or running records informally with deaf children, as described in Chapter 3. Also, retelling (Chapter 3) might be used in place of questions or "discussion" to assess comprehension.

Page 4: Writing samples (writing in English and other community languages) to include children's earliest attempts at writing (pp. 50-54)

The last page of the Observations and Samples form is similar to page three but documents assessment information about writing. As with the reading sample, this page is completed with comments about a single sample of a child's writing. The sample of writing used for this observation should be attached to the form. Also, similar to the reading sample, the *Handbook* suggests filling out this page once a term (twice a year) or photocopying it for more frequent use (p. 50). The prompts for this page, again, written in boldface, are provided below (p. 50):

1. **Context and background information about writing**
    - Prompts teachers to include information about the following: context of the writing (was the child alone, the nature of the task, how it was approached, etc.); the kind of writing (genre); and whether the writing was an extract of longer work, a draft, or a finished product.

2. **Child's own response to the writing**

    - Suggests that children's comments before, during, or after the writing be recorded.

3. **Teacher's response**
    - Indicates that teachers should respond to the content, the student's ability to handle the form of the genre, and form an overall impression of the writing.

4. **Development of spelling and conventions of writing**

5. **What this writing shows about the child's development as a writer**

    - Prompts teachers to indicate how this sample "fits into the range of previous writing and the kind of support/experience needed for further development" (ref. p. 54).

The Observations and Samples form from the PLR—all four pages—fits with teachers' needs to record the descriptive information obtained with alternative assessment procedures. Additionally, it fulfills the need for day-to-day assessment to lead back to a longitudinal understanding of a child's development, as described in Chapter 3. For example, this form guides teachers to record information about different areas of literacy—the same areas indicated by the components of the Stages of Literacy Development described in Chapter 2 and included in **Appendix A**. In this way, teachers are prepared—with documentation of observational information as well as other forms of assessment—to summarize a child's development of literacy holistically and relate the information to stages of development.

A final note about the Observations and Samples form—the *Handbook* suggests that teachers use this form in flexible ways to meet their own needs, including photocopying parts of the form for more frequent use (p. 55). There are other suggestions as well. For example, teachers might prefer to copy and separate the pages of the form and maintain records of samples and the diaries in separate places. The diary of talking and listening (conversation) might be kept close at hand during activities—perhaps on a clipboard or taped to the wall. Some teachers, as described in the *Handbook*, clip out the headings and prompts from the forms and use them as part of their own record-keeping systems (p. 56). The point here is that the system provides guidance and structure for maintaining records of observational information. The way a teacher uses the system, however, is an individual decision.

Teachers' Files: As indicated earlier, teachers need a place to store their own assessment information and contributions of information from other sources. Maintaining a file for each student's progress in literacy for the year is an easy way to add data as it is collected. "File" here should be interpreted loosely, as suggested earlier regarding students' files. The receptacle should be appropriate for collecting varied examples of learning, including videotapes and artwork. Teachers will need to access these files frequently to add information, sort and review the information, and use it to make instructional decisions. This information also will support collections of data recorded at the end of the year at the program level, described next.

Examples of Teacher's File Contents[11]

- copies of items from students' files or portfolios;

---

[11] Contents will vary according to students' development, interests, and literacy activities.

- anecdotal notes, from class observations as well as observations of work, both process and product—see Observations and Samples form;

- holistic writing assessments (descriptive and/or scores);

- reading assessments (retelling descriptions/scores, informal reading inventory results, informal miscue analysis results)—see Observations and Samples form;

- checklists (Developmental, P-Levels, informal reading and writing),

- paper-and-pencil test scores;

- copies of self-interest surveys;

- notes from parent conversations, surveys, interviews, etc.; and

- notes from staff reviews about the student.

Record Keeping at the Program Level

Record keeping at this level serves multiple purposes and should be designed collaboratively by all who use the information. To guide instruction in the coming year, the system should profile students' development of literacy at the end of the current year in a way that communicates this information—patterns of strengths and needs—to others. This profile, developed by the teacher, should be filed with supporting evidence. "Evidence" here includes assessment data gathered by the teacher and information from other contexts and sources (e.g., standardized test scores, assessments or reports contributed by others who work with the child). Teachers should use this additional information, along with records of classroom assessments, in developing students' profiles. Those designing records at this level should plan the form of the profile and decide how it, and supporting information, will be maintained.

The procedures and tools of record keeping at this level should be standardized for two reasons. First, because these records are used by all members of the program, they should reflect the way the educational community views literacy. In fact, they can and should contribute to building a consistent perspective on the development of literacy within the program. Second, because they should demonstrate long-term growth, records at this level must maintain a degree of consistency in the way in which that growth is assessed and recorded by those who work with the same student over time.

Decisions about the organization of record keeping at this level should flow from a developmental view of literacy. Stages of development as well as all areas of literacy should be represented (communicative competency, social interactions, motivation, text knowledge and strategy use, background knowledge, concepts and forms of writing, and writing process skills). However, this developmental perspective also implies that there would be differences in the kinds of information recorded for students at different levels of development. These differences have to do with the focus of assessment (what information is collected and how) as well as the types of assessment data—observational vs. measurement. For example, assessment of younger children and those at lower levels of development should be almost entirely (if not completely) observational and represent a focus on development of competence in conversational language and emerging skills in other areas of literacy.

Provided below are examples of record keeping at the program level for the needs described above—to develop a profile for each student and to maintain a file that contains this form and supporting assessment information. A sample profile form that was designed to accompany the Stages of Literacy Development is included in **Appendix A-1**. A literacy notebook (Rhodes & Shanklin, 1993) is suggested as a way to maintain assessment profiles and supporting data at this level. Finally, the PLR (Barrs et al., 1988) is mentioned as another example of an assessment profile.

Literacy Assessment Profiles: As described in Chapter 3 and mentioned in other places in this text, day-to-day classroom assessment must support the development of a summary of progress at the end of each academic year. This summary should be more than a snapshot of the child's functioning at the time. It should describe development in a way that is consistent with previous summaries and with the summaries that will follow in future years. Specifically, the assessment profile should be consistent with principles of assessment described throughout this book—e.g., that literacy should be examined holistically (include information about language, reading, and writing); that it should be examined developmentally and as a collaborative process (one that involves others); and that it should address all areas within development (e.g., components in the Stages of Literacy Development). An assessment profile should include the following items.

- Student's age, the year, teacher(s);
- Language(s) used by the student conversationally (understood and expressed);
- Information about degree of competency in conversational language(s);
- Information about a student's approximate stage of development of literacy: Emerging, Beginning, Developing, or Maturing (considering communicative competency, reading, and writing);

- Student's current reading level (instructional and independent) and average holistic writing score (based on a standardized scoring procedure), if appropriate; and
- Description of student's strengths, needs, and recommendations for instruction, considering all areas of literacy (conversational language and written language).

The profile, of course, would be supported with evidence obtained through assessment. This points back to the need to have procedures and tools for obtaining the data as well as records of assessment at other levels to draw upon. The effectiveness of the profile depends upon the quality of the assessments used and the records maintained of the results.

The relationship between a child's age, proficiency in conversational language, stage of development, and level of reading comprehension (as applies) provide an initial impression of a child's current status in literacy development. For example, consider the following hypothetical profile:

> **Student's age:** 10
> **Communicative Competency:** P-Level 4 (Kendall Communicative
> > Proficiency Levels assessment of Communicative Competency
> > Level, **Appendix B**);
> **Stage of Literacy Development:** Beginning Level (Stages of Literacy
> > Development, **Appendix A**);
> **Reading Comprehension:** end of first grade (see Guidelines for
> > Determining Reading Grade Level, **Appendix E**)

The discrepancies between this student's age, conversational language competency, literacy level, and reading comprehension are significant. It would probably be safe to assume, based on this information alone, that the student needs programming (long-term goals) that will give priority to conversational language development. Prioritizing this area over instruction in written language (reading and writing) would be consistent with a developmental perspective—one that addresses previously unmet goals of development first. It would not be appropriate, in other words, to center instruction in reading and writing until the student reaches higher levels of conversational language competency. It is important, too, that this student's learning in all other areas is not being channeled primarily through printed sources of information.

The assessment profile should include guidelines for describing a student's strengths, needs, and recommendations for instruction. These should be based on a developmental perspective and take into consideration the areas of the development of literacy discussed in Chapter 2 (components of Stages of Literacy Development). Sample guidelines are shown below:

Individual Literacy Profile

Strengths: *Describe significant progress the student has made or ongoing strengths that have enabled him or her to progress* either within the current stage of development or to a higher stage. Consider different types of learning (e.g., knowledge, behavior, attitudes) and areas of development (e.g., text knowledge/comprehension strategies, communicative competency, motivation) For example, a student might be progressing primarily because he or she is highly motivated to read and spends a great deal of free time reading.

Needs: *Describe the types of learning (knowledge, behavior, or attitudes) the student has not yet acquired but needs in order to progress* within his or her level of development or to a higher level of development. Needs may originate from previous levels of development or from the present level of functioning.

Recommendations for Instruction: *Describe recommendations for instruction based on needs*, described above, *priorities for instructional focus*—areas to target for long-term goals, and suggestions for *approaches or strategies that are effective* with the student.

As mentioned, a sample profile form was developed to accompany the Stages of Literacy Development and is included in **Appendix A-1.** The completed PLR is another example of an assessment profile. Any assessment profile form, and the procedures for completing the form, should result in the following:

▶ a summary of a child's development of literacy that includes information about both conversational and written language,

▶ information that reflects the input of others—parents, the child, and others who work with the child—obtained with formal, defined procedures, and

▶ narrative descriptions of the child's progress based heavily on observational, alternative assessments.

The assessments used should be documented to support the profile. The Optional Samples and Record form of the PLR, described earlier, is an example of how observational assessment information might be documented.

Literacy Assessment Notebook: As explained, there needs to be a system at the program level for maintaining students' profiles and supporting data over time. Literacy Assessment Notebooks (Rhodes & Shanklin, 1993) can be used for that purpose. These notebooks, or another suitable container, include selections chosen by the teachers from their files, the students' files, or their portfolios. A form similar to the Observations and Records form might include anecdotal notes and samples of observational assessment. Students could assist in making selections from their files or portfolios that best indicate their progress during the year. Contributions to the notebook will typically be made at the end of the year as teachers prepare a profile of the students' progress for the current year. However, teachers may indicate items that should be included from their files throughout the year.

Records maintained at this level also include information contributed from sources other than the teachers' and students' assessment records. Other professionals who work with a student and conduct their own assessments will contribute to its contents. Keeping the notebook in a central location will make it easier for all professional staff members to access the information as they need it. The Literacy Assessment Notebook pulls together information from all sources of assessment data. Listed below are examples of the contents:

Examples of Literacy Assessment Notebook Contents:[16]

- student profile—discussions of strengths, needs, and instructional recommendations based on teacher's classroom assessments, including supporting assessment information such as the following:
   - tools that provide detail about competencies according to stages of development (e.g., Stages of Literacy Development used as a checklist, **Appendix A**),
   - Communicative Competency assessment checklists, language samples, etc. (e.g., P-Levels, **Appendix B**),
   end-of-year checklists for reading and writing with notes (e.g., reading checklists, **Appendix C**),
   - student-selected portfolio items with comments,
   - end-of-year holistic writing scores and sample, with comments (e.g., KDES Writing Levels, **Appendix D**), and
   - selected teacher-made tests;

- end-of-year reading/writing lists (books read, types of writing explored);

- end-of-year interest/self-assessment inventory;

---

[16] Contents will vary according to students' development, interests, and literacy activities.

- standardized test scores, with comments;

- notes from parent discussions;

- reports, test scores, and interpretations from specialists; and

- reports from educational team reviews about the student.

In summary, individuals in the educational system need tools for documenting and recording assessment information for different purposes. At each level, the tools or methods should suit the needs of the primary users—students, teachers, and others in the educational system. Further, the primary users should maintain and control assessment records at the different levels. At the program level, this is a collaborative effort. A comprehensive record-keeping system documents information that points to students' strengths, instructional needs, and long-term patterns of development. However, the effectiveness of the system depends on the definition of the tools for record keeping and on the way in which they are used, as described below.

The Assessment Process

The record-keeping system described thus far adds to the information about assessment in the preceding chapters. It also alludes to the *process* of assessment. The process of assessment must be defined in order to put into effect the information discussed in this and previous chapters: tools for record keeping, systems for involving others in assessment, the implementation of classroom assessment methods, and the development of instructional goals based on profiles of students. This process involves coordinating assessment at different levels—with different individuals and for different purposes. It also involves determining the timing of various assessment events. Some of this is indicated with record keeping, as exemplified with the PLR (Barrs et al., 1988), described in the previous chapter. However, this process should be defined at all levels and for all purposes: the students,' the teachers,' and at the program level. Below is an example of how the assessment process might flow during an academic year from a teacher's perspective. The nature of the assessments used would, of course, vary depending upon the student.

Assessment Process During the Academic Year	
Fall	**Assessments used:**
Review stages and supporting assessment information from previous years in Literacy Notebooks for strengths, needs, suggestions for instruction from previous academic year, and patterns of development over time.	Literacy Notebooks Individual Student Profiles (Chapter 5)
Review long-term goals for students and initial short-term goals based on the information above and other sources of curricular goals (these goals should already be determined with previous year assessments and stated in the profile).	Stages of Literacy Development (Chapter 2)
Collect initial assessment information from students and parents (e.g., Primary Language Record); use this to support or revise goals.	Conferences, Self-assessments (Chapter 4)
Establish systems for record keeping and initial methods of assessment: files, checklists, methods for documenting observational information, etc.	Teacher files Selected methods of assessment, determined with goals (Chapters 3 & 5)
Establish, collaboratively with students, student files and portfolios; determine how others (parents, other educational staff) will be involved in portfolio assessment; communicate portfolio process to others.	Student files Portfolios Conferences (Chapters 3 and 4)
Continue to Assess Short-term Goals for Instruction Daily	**See Chapter 3**
Continue to Assess at Regular Intervals (e.g., quarterly, monthly) Throughout the Year	**Assessments used:**
Structure time and assist students in reviewing their files, making selections for portfolios according to goals (established in previous conferences), and conducting self-assessments.	Student files Portfolios Self-assessments (Chapter 4)
Review portfolio contents; assess items with appropriately selected methods (e.g., use holistic scoring procedures to assess writing; rubrics to assess other work).	Informal observations Selected assessment tools or procedures
Confer with others on selected items from portfolios (e.g., parents respond to portfolio as determined in the fall, colleagues assess selected items)	Conferences or other forms of communication

Confer with colleagues about students' progress (e.g., may be as part of portfolio assessment or may address other areas of progress, other assessments).	Educational Review Meetings (Chapter 4)
Discuss portfolio progress according to input from all sources with students; review & reconstruct portfolio goals (may include other forms of self-assessment in this process).	Conferences
Review records for each student for the quarter, including assessment information collected from all sources (teacher, student, colleagues, parents); review this according to long-term goals; reconstruct goals as necessary.	Teacher files Stages of Literacy Development
Spring	**Assessments used:**
Perform end-of-year assessments, including assessment of communicative competency (e.g., P-Levels, Appendix B), holistic writing assessments for level of functioning (e.g., KDES writing levels, Appendix D), and independent reading comprehension level (Appendix E); include colleagues in these assessments.	Selected assessment procedures and tools
Confer with colleagues about students' progress; obtain information based on their assessments as well as contributions they make to joint assessments (e.g., P-Levels).	Educational Review Meetings
Obtain additional self-assessment information from students.	Self-assessments
Confer with parents and students about progress.	Conferences
Review portfolio progress (may be used as the forum for conferring with colleagues, parents, students, previously indicated).	Portfolios
Consolidate information above (data from different sources) in teacher files for students.	Teacher files
Review teacher file information for each student. Decide approximate level of development and patterns of development determined by competencies in various areas (e.g., Stages of Literacy Development, Appendix A).	Stages of Literacy Development (Chapter 2)
Use this and supporting assessment information to develop student profile (e.g., could be developed with form such as Primary Language Record); profile is developed with input from others (as indicated above) and verified by others.	Student profile

Select from class files (including items copied from portfolios) data that best supports information in the profile (e.g., may include form similar to Observation and Sample form from the Primary Language Record for documentation of observational information).	Teacher files
Include profile and supporting assessment data in Literacy Notebook.	Literacy Notebook Student profile

Although there are many steps to the assessment process, in practice it should be efficient and manageable for those involved. Both the tools and the process should be planned in advance as much as possible, and new procedures should be implemented slowly. Furthermore, the overall framework should indicate the ways in which different levels of record keeping, such as those kept by students, support the records at another level, such as the teachers' files. At the end of the year, the process should culminate with collections of data, of various types and from different sources, that enable teachers to make valid statements about their students' progress in literacy for the academic year.

Conclusion

A system of record keeping and a definition of the process are as important as the selection and use of assessment methods. Record keeping must be planned at different levels for different needs: students' needs to maintain records of their progress, teachers' needs to record information about each student for the year, and the program's needs to have documentation of students' progress across years to reflect a longitudinal perspective on development. Information at each of these levels guides instruction; a weakness in the system at any one level lessens the effectiveness with which assessment can carry out this task.

Record keeping must align with instruction to support the assessment-instruction link. If instruction and assessment are approached developmentally and holistically, then record keeping needs to reflect this perspective. The PLR (Barrs et al., 1988) is an example of record keeping that supports these concepts and others described in Chapter 1. For example, the PLR examines conversational and written language as interrelated areas of development. It reflects the tie between evaluation and instruction through the use of observational assessment in authentic literacy activities. It also reflects this tie with recommendations for instruction. By involving others in assessment, it represents a comprehensive and balanced assessment program. What's more, by

A record-keeping system such as this may be used for its intended purposes and as a basis for staff and program development in issues of literacy. That purpose is discussed in the preface of the *Handbook* for the PLR. A clearly articulated framework of language and the development of literacy, demonstrated in tools and procedures for record keeping at all levels of the instructional system, "is a good starting point for staff discussions, the development of school policies, and for curriculum planning" (Barrs et al., 1988, preface). This is another example of how assessment might guide instruction.

On that note, this chapter closes by emphasizing a word of advice: Where record-keeping systems do not exist, or should be changed, start slowly. Take time to add new techniques in ways that are not overwhelming. Establish procedures for maintaining student files before adding portfolios. Document observations of one student at a time, or several students in one activity. Begin portfolio assessment with a few students and add more later. Determine program-level needs collaboratively, through discussion. Realize, too, that record keeping conducted as a mutual effort of shared responsibility is less burdensome than a system implemented by one person.

Chapter 6

Planning for Literacy Instruction

Considering Methods and Approaches

Guidelines for Planning and Instruction for Literacy

Conclusion

Planning for Literacy Instruction

*For years, in fact almost two centuries, we have searched for the key to the language education of deaf children... As I review the various approaches and perspectives...utilized today in the education of deaf children, I want to emphasize that **no single** (emphasis added) one of these holds the key...*

(Fischgrund, 1996, p. 2)

There is a belief that the pursuit of better methods of instruction leads to or has led to the improvement of achievement in literacy. The point, of course, is to remedy the deficiencies of text-based literacy in children and adolescents who are deaf...many educators might not even be aware of the growing consensus that the notion of good or bad methods is itself misguided.

(Paul, 1998, p. 140)

There are many opinions about the best approach to instructing deaf children in literacy. Often these opinions reveal themselves in the methods or approaches programs use to improve the quality of instruction. Students benefit in varying degrees from practices based on many of these methods. Just as often, however, the methods fail to bring about the expected significant differences in achievement, in both individuals and groups of students. One of the reasons for this could be that educators often look to individual methods or approaches as the "key" that will open the door to deaf children's achievement in literacy. When one approach does not result in significant, anticipated changes in achievement, energy is invested in another approach or method. However, as indicated with the quotes on the previous page, there is in fact no such key or best method. The task of improving deaf children's literacy must be approached with multiple, interdependent goals organized over time. The results should help define educational practices that are effective with specific students or groups of students.

The goal of this chapter is to indicate that methodology is second to individual need. It is the *flexible* use of methods based on the needs of individual children that determines instructional effectiveness. Deciding how to use methods, given this premise, should be directed with a set of guidelines that are congruent with theories about learning for language, literacy, and deaf children. Planning for literacy starts with these theories and guidelines. Methods, approaches, and even models of instruction should follow, defining how programs will carry out these basic guidelines.

The chapter begins by examining selected methods and approaches to literacy instruction, citing ways that these might benefit students—or not—depending upon implementation. That section is followed by seven guidelines for planning literacy instruction, based on the same broad theories about learning that support the principles of assessment described in Chapter 1. This section on instruction presents guidelines, strategies, and tools for assessing deaf children's language and literacy development. Readers are advised to remember the interdependency of these guidelines—that each supports the implementation and effectiveness of the others. The chapter closes with a reminder, too, that the guidelines, and all planning for literacy, should be considered within the broader context of educational goals and within the social context of learning for each individual.

Considering Methods and Approaches

In reality, any one approach or method can either work in ways that benefit students in their pursuit of literacy or can serve to work against their development. Take, for example, the following list of approaches that might be used to improve instruction for literacy:

1. Select the best curriculum or commercial reading and writing program.

2. Hire the best teachers.

3. Focus more instructional time and energy on reading and writing.

4. Use better diagnostics and remedial strategies to improve reading and writing skills.

5. Immerse children in good literature.

6. Spend more time on the direct instruction of English language and reading skills.

7. Converse with students in American Sign Language (ASL) socially and in academic contexts.

8. Develop bilingual programs (ASL as the first language, written English as the second).

Benefits and Cautions

Each of the above approaches, as described below, has potential merits and drawbacks, depending on how it is applied.

1. Select the best curriculum or commercial reading and writing program.

Benefits: Commercial materials and curricula can be a source of information for instructional guidelines and ideas for activities. Furthermore, many commercial programs now include excellent children's literature, with the stories arranged according to approximate grade levels. This information is helpful in matching materials to a child's appropriate reading level.

Cautions: When programs invest heavily in finding the "best" program to use, they may be perceiving these materials as the primary source of instructional information and the answer to their instructional difficulties. This often leads to doggedly following the program's sequence of skills for instructional goals, rather than using assessment information about students' developmental strengths and needs. As discussed in earlier chapters, relying on commercial or other curricular materials as the primary source of instructional goals may present problems for the following reasons: 1) there may be a mismatch between individual development and these goals; 2) commercial materials base instruction on assumptions about children—their communicative competency, background knowledge, and early experiences in literacy (in other words, many students, deaf *and* hearing, do not fit the implied profile); and 3) commercial materials represent a skill-sequenced view of learning that does not accurately reflect the complexity of literacy—both the interdependency of multiple areas of development and the holistic nature of that development.

2. Hire the best teachers.

Benefits: Certain teachers seem to stand out for their instructional expertise. These teachers usually have high expectations for their students; implement well-structured, creative, programs; and tend to bring out the best in their students. There is no doubt that a child benefits from having a teacher like this—one who knows how to capitalize on his or her students' strengths and effectively address instructional needs.

Cautions: Teachers' styles and personalities vary, often making even the best teachers more effective for some students than for others. These differences should be taken into account. Teachers' effectiveness, however, ultimately should be measured according to the goal of facilitating students' long-term development—the cumulative effects of years of teaching and planning—rather than the degree of success any one teacher has within a single year. Within the same program, teachers bring to the task of instruction different paradigms about learning and the development of literacy—beliefs that influence the way they teach and assess. As a result, teachers may be considered "good" at their job to the degree that they share paradigms with those passing judgment. Consequently, it is possible for a student to have a good teacher one year and a good teacher the next year, according to different opinions about teaching and learning, and yet experience vastly different approaches to instruction. When that happens, instructional inconsistency within a program can fail to build students' development over time. It is hard for students to make gains over time, or beyond the current year, if there is little continuity within the program in its approaches to instruction.

3. Focus more instructional time and energy on reading and writing.

Benefits: There should be a well-balanced program for reading and writing for all students, with structured activities occurring daily. The form of these activities will change as students mature, gradually incorporating more guided instruction in reading and writing within the context of authentic reading and writing tasks. Students need more time on these tasks and less time on isolated skill exercises.

Cautions: There are at least three ways in which this approach can ultimately fail students. First of all, it could represent an approach that narrowly defines literacy as text-based skills, or competence in reading and writing. Focusing literacy instruction on reading and writing alone will defeat the purpose of spending more time developing these skills if related areas of development (e.g., conversational language, motivation, etc.) are neglected. A second way this approach might fail is if large blocks of time are devoted to instruction in reading and writing, but the instruction is devoid of subject matter from other curricular areas. A third way of misusing this approach is by increasing time spent on paper-and-pencil exercises that do not involve students in the actual tasks of reading and writing.

4. Use better diagnostics and remedial strategies to improve reading and writing skills.

Benefits: Most of this book stresses the concept that assessment is important to instruction in literacy. The first chapter points out that assessment should find out what a student knows, what skills he or she has, and what his or her instructional needs are in order to plan effective instruction.

Cautions: The words used in this assumption connote the need for caution. The terms "diagnostic" and "remedial" often represent approaches to instruction based on the view that if students do not have certain skills and knowledge by a certain grade or age, then something is wrong with them—they have a problem that must be diagnosed and fixed (Johnston & Allington, 1991). Such approaches are not developmental and may be counterproductive to instructional efforts. Developmental perspectives view growth in literacy as a matter of individual course, varying in pattern according to a students' strengths and needs at any given time. Assessment focuses on determining these instructional strengths and needs rather than "diagnosing" the problem. While this may seem like a matter of semantics, the developmental perspective carries a more positive outlook that is likely to filter down to the student, influencing his or her own self-perceptions and motivation to learn.

5. Immerse children in good literature.

Benefits: Independent reading—reading for pleasure—is a critical factor in helping many children learn to read and write, whether they are deaf or hearing. What children learn as a result of developing this habit will *far* outweigh any amount or kind of instruction they receive. Independent reading provides students with abundant comprehensible input about written English—more than they can ever hope to learn through instruction (Krashen, 1992). The development of this habit starts early when young children experience the pleasures of looking at books and being read to by others. Emphasizing a love for good literature, both at home and in school, facilitates the acquisition of this habit.

Cautions: Many readers are aware that this assumption has been taken to the extreme in some instructional programs for deaf, and even hearing, children. Often children do acquire a knowledge of reading and writing naturally—in fact, all do to some degree—but most do not learn to read and write this way exclusively. They need guided instruction in these skills. Instruction, moreover, is a matter of finding the right balance between creating conditions that foster acquisition (such as immersing children in good literature) and learning through purposeful demonstration and explicit explanation of the features of language and concepts of literacy.

6. Spend more time on the direct instruction of English language and reading skills.

Benefits: Research has indicated many areas and contexts in which direct instruction can improve areas of development in literacy. For example, the literature on strategy use, described later in this chapter, indicates there are strategies that good readers use to comprehend text that can be made explicit to poor readers with direct explanation (e.g., Baker & Brown, 1984; Garner, 1987; Paris, Wasik, Turner, 1991; Pressley, Johnson, Symons, McGoldrick, & Kurita, 1989). Also, deaf students who have not acquired competence in conversational language during early childhood need instruction in language in addition to continued efforts that support acquisition.

Cautions: Just as there is research indicating the benefits of direct instruction, there is also research indicating situations in which this is not the case. When rules about language—grammar instruction—are taught out of context and assumed to transfer to reading and writing, for example, this transfer does not appear to occur (Krashen, 1984). Demonstration and direct instruction are most likely to be effective when used to teach skills and strategies *as needed* (e.g., developmentally appropriate) and within the context of authentic reading and writing activities. Furthermore, instruction must include the application of learned skills and strategies in multiple contexts. Direct instruction involves thoughtful consideration of what to teach, when, and how.

7. Converse with students in ASL socially and in academic contexts.

Benefits: Conversing with students in ASL for social and academic purposes is increasingly recognized as important to the education of many deaf children (e.g., Israelite et al., 1989; Johnson et al., 1989; Lane, 1992; Mahshie, 1995). As the natural language of deaf people in this country, ASL—its acquisition and use—allows deaf children, the majority of whom need a visual language, to experience conversational language for all the purposes for which language is intended. In addition, the early acquisition and use of this language builds a knowledge base, both of language and concepts, that supports further learning. The use of ASL also represents cultural recognition for many students, undoubtedly boosting self-esteem and motivation—critical affective variables in the development of literacy. Those who need a visual language and grow up in an environment that is rich in the conversational use of ASL are likely to have language skills and knowledge that will assist their development in many ways.

Cautions: Decisions about language use should always take into account the linguistic needs and preferences of the individual child. The goal of language choice is to provide accessible input and to facilitate early acquisition (Mahshie, 1995). Therefore, for each child with a hearing loss, assessment should aim to determine the language and conditions that will best meet that goal. In addition to whether the child needs visual access to language—which will be true for the vast majority of those with severe to profound hearing loss—two questions must be asked: 1) "Is the child acquiring a solid basis in the intended language (whether it be ASL or spoken English)?" and 2) "How can the conditions for providing the input necessary for early acquisition be provided?" The child's language and the environment must be continuously assessed in answer to these questions. Furthermore, decisions about the choice of language and conditions should be monitored routinely throughout the child's development in literacy—well beyond the preschool years. Significant delays in a child's development should be noted and prompt a review of the choice of language and the conditions for learning.

Even when students clearly need the visual input of ASL, this language—or any language—can be used in ways that are incomprehensible if individual needs are not taken into account. Language development varies greatly among deaf students, a fact that is influenced further by the diversity of language approaches used in the United States. For example, when students change programs or enter a program for the first time as older students, their language base may be very different from their new classmates, both in kind and degree of proficiency. These new students may have unique language needs that prevent them from coping with classroom conversations until they have further developed ASL through acquisition or instruction. Their language needs must be addressed with individual planning.

8. Develop bilingual programs (ASL as the first language, written English as the second).

Benefits: Bilingual programs have come about as a result of recognizing ASL as a true, visually accessible language and increasing its use in the classroom (e.g., Lane, 1992). Since there is no written form of ASL, however, students still need to learn to read and write English. This has led to the development of bilingual/ESL (English as a Second Language) programs based on the concept that students will learn ASL as a first language and English as a second language. Bilingual programs vary in their implementation and their goals, both in this country and abroad. While it is generally true that ASL is learned as the first language and English as the second, some students, such as those with moderate hearing losses, may learn spoken English as a first language but continue to learn and use ASL for the visual access it provides for learning. Many students in these programs learn English exclusively through print; others may learn spoken English as well, but ASL is the language of instruction for all. These programs are often referred to as bilingual/bicultural because of their strong emphasis on cultural affiliation. In fact, advocates of these programs may not view bilingual education as an *approach* to instruction, but instead as the natural progression of literacy development for deaf children (Hansen & Mosqueira, 1995).

In bilingual programs, ASL is used for social and academic purposes and as a linguistic support for learning English, the second language. Beginning very early, distinctions are made between the use of the two languages. With young children, this happens in developmentally appropriate activities that build language knowledge and skill indirectly (Erting & Phau, 1997). As students become older and better able to reflect on their knowledge of language use, the structures of each may be explored in more detail, typically using ASL to explain features of English, the lesser known language. Bilingual programs stress the need to develop competence in ASL before providing *formal* instruction in English. They do, however, advocate engaging deaf children in the same literacy-rich early childhood activities that many hearing children experience (e.g., Erting, 1997; Mahshie, 1995).

These programs enable many students to use their conversational language strengths in ASL and their conceptual knowledge gained through this language to further their learning in literacy and all other curricular areas. The potential benefits of bilingual programming include early competence in conversational language, a more timely acquisition of knowledge in all areas, advancement in the written skills of literacy as a second language, and cultural identification which influences self-esteem.

Cautions: It is possible for a program to claim to be "bilingual" but still fail at instruction in literacy for a variety of other reasons, including its interpretation of bilingual instruction. For example, efforts to develop ASL prior to written English could be interpreted by some in ways that might limit young children's early, natural experiences involving print. Many concepts about the uses of print are acquired during the preschool years through these natural activities.

Other factors that must be in place before bilingual programs can reach their goals include: adequate numbers of staff who are fluent in both languages and knowledgeable of the structures of both; training for staff in second-language acquisition, steps to ensure congruence between instruction and cultural mores (Nover & Andrews, 1998; Woodward, 1978); and support for families—especially those that do not already know and use ASL—beginning with the birth of the deaf child.

Of major importance to the success of these programs, too, is continued research into the development and education of this unique group of students. No other group of students has the educational goal of developing competency in two languages used in different modes. Efforts such as the *Star Schools Project*, under the direction of Steve Nover (1998), are needed to define, implement, and test bilingual/ESL models of instruction in the United States. In fact, multiple projects of this kind are needed to study bilingual programs with different populations of deaf children in this country—models that prove effective for one group of students may prove less effective for another.

Summary

Apart from their individual merits and possible misuses, approaches to improving instruction in literacy may fail to bring about more positive results for several common reasons. First of all, as indicated earlier, educators may see an individual approach as a solution to improving achievement in literacy and put all of their educational energy and resources into implementing this one approach. Second, any approach can be implemented without due consideration of students' individual needs and developmental patterns, thus failing a number of students. Third, educators may interpret any approach to improving literacy achievement with a narrow focus on teaching text-based skills—reading and writing—and not adopt a broader view of development in this area. Further, the goal of literacy achievement using any method may be approached in ways that are out of proportion and even incompatible with students' overarching educational needs.

For the approaches above, and others, to be effective, educators must use them in flexible, multidimensional ways with individual students. They must succeed in establishing conditions for learning over time, both in the home and at school, in collaborative efforts involving many individuals. These conditions must foster progress on many interdependent fronts, not just reading and writing, in the development of literacy. When instructional approaches and methods are implemented within this context—with a child-centered view of the development of literacy—they have a greater potential to succeed. One should measure their success according to students' progress over time, not by the extent to which a program implements a particular method.

In other words, methods, strategies, and approaches do not come first in planning and instruction for literacy. Neither should they alone determine any child's programming. Rather, the selection of these—and the implementation of each—should be guided by principles, similar to the way choices about assessment should be made. Furthermore, the principles for instruction should come from the same theories about learning and development of literacy for deaf children that support assessment. They should take into account the active, reflective nature of learning; the holistic, affective, and social aspects of development; and the multiple intelligences of the learners. If the potential benefits and cautions of the approaches and methods discussed above were analyzed for supporting principles, they would probably point to the following guidelines.

Guidelines for Planning and Instruction for Literacy

The seven guidelines discussed here originate from information about the theories of learning in Chapter 1 and the development of literacy in Chapter 2. They represent conditions that deaf children need with regard to literacy acquisition, learning, and instruction. Hopefully, also, they indicate areas where educators should put their efforts into both defining related practices and implementing them.

When reading these guidelines, one should keep in mind that they are interdependent. Each interlocks with the other in a way that requires consistency in how they are applied to individuals. Further, that consistency must be sustained across the program for students. In order to achieve this goal, those involved in the educational planning, including parents, need to reach consensus in their interpretation of these guidelines and what they mean for individual students. For that reason, programs should invest time in discussing theories of learning and the development of literacy that support these guidelines, and their application to individual students.

While guidelines are presented as questions addressing planning for literacy, they do not impact classroom instruction alone. In many cases, they point to the need for establishing conditions both within the educational community and in the home. Also, these questions should not be answered once and considered resolved for individual students. They should be revisited according to students' progress throughout development. In other words, they should contribute to a "living" curriculum for each child as he or she grows and changes with development. As mentioned, the degree to which these guidelines—and resulting practices—effectively foster development *over time* determines the success of an individual child's literacy program.

1. **Do planning and instruction take into account a broad view of literacy and the interdependency of various areas of development: conversational language, motivation (affect), social interactions, and background knowledge in addition to text-based skills (reading and writing)?**

   A broad view of literacy includes planning for *dimensions* of learning (Syverson, 1995), including the development of conversational language and literate thought as well as the text-based skills of reading and writing. Students must acquire a base of knowledge (non-strategic) about the world around them, including language, as well as strategic knowledge they can use to solve problems and further their own learning (Pressley, Goodchild, Fleet, &

Zajchowski, 1989). A broad view of literacy demonstrates awareness of the *interdependency* of areas within literacy development: communicative competency, text knowledge and strategic use, social interaction, background knowledge, and motivation. It is unlikely that the text-based skills of reading and writing will develop in isolation from its associated variables.

2. **Are planning and instruction based on developmental information—the assessment of individual patterns of growth according to universal stages of language and development of literacy beyond the current year? Does instruction address both the strengths and needs of students within their present stage of functioning as well as continuing needs from previous stages of development?**

Children progress in their development of literacy in unique, uneven patterns of strengths and learning needs in related areas of growth. Over time, however, learning conforms to a recognized sequence of broad stages of development in which major tasks or areas of learning are achieved. Achievement of these major tasks is necessary for further development. Instruction should facilitate meeting these goals. However, children do not need instruction in skills and knowledge they already possess nor can they acquire skills and knowledge for which they are not ready developmentally. Further, as discussed under the previous guideline, their progress is likely to be impeded when critical areas do not develop in conjunction with others. As a result, the most effective instruction will be that which addresses current needs, as determined through assessment—including those from earlier stages as well as those within the present stage of development. Teachers can best respond to students' needs by capitalizing on their related strengths—their skills, knowledge, interests, and attitudes.

3. **Is conversational language accessible, used in a variety of ways, and are students engaged in meaningful dialogue as much as possible? Is this language represented fully, clearly, and consistently? Does this occur in all environments, not just in a single classroom, and from year to year in a students' program?**

One of the earliest decisions about a deaf child's needs regarding literacy concerns how to make conversational language accessible and comprehensible. The importance of acquiring language in early childhood has been described in Chapter 2. For most deaf children, the natural answer to this question is to use a visual language, ASL. The decision about language accessibility does not stop here, however. In order for language to be accessible and comprehensible, it must be *fully, clearly, and consistently represented in multiple contexts and over time.* Children must be able to interact with others who are proficient in the language

—native users of the language—in age-appropriate ways. It is important for those involved in a deaf child's development to recognize these related issues concerning language choice. If the conditions for representing and receiving language—whether spoken or signed—cannot be met, then language is not accessible. Recognizing how difficult it is to establish these conditions in some cases for a variety of reasons, this guideline should serve as a goal and a reminder of the importance of early and full-fledged language acquisition. It should not be used to justify language choice based on adult preference or proficiency instead of a child's needs. Nor should this principle be used to deter efforts on the part of anyone to communicate with a deaf child, whether that person is proficient in the child's language or not.

4. Does instruction reflect awareness of the languages used by the students—both according to purpose and degree of competence? Are instructional strategies used that are consistent with this awareness?

Related to the preceding guideline, it is important to identify what language or languages children are learning, and for what purposes (e.g., conversation, reading, and writing). Clarifying language use is necessary for establishing goals for the learning of literacy. It also should define the instructional process for literacy as well as for other areas of learning. For example, Peter V. Paul's book *Literacy and Deafness* (1998) has two consecutive chapters titled "Instruction and First Language Literacy," and "Instruction and Second Language Literacy." The first refers to situations in which deaf children are learning to read and write English as the same language they use conversationally. The second title refers to those in which students are learning to read and write English as a different language from the one they use conversationally. (Paul makes the point that references to second-language literacy for deaf children usually assume ASL to be the first language; this assumption overlooks the possibility that students, especially those from other minority cultures, may have some degree of knowledge of other spoken languages.) In these chapters, Paul describes separate approaches to instruction based on these differences. If the learning of literacy involves two languages, students' competencies in the first language should be used to support learning in the lesser known, second language. Strategies for implementing this are described in Paul (1998) and in other publications describing second-language literacy for deaf students (e.g., Mahshie, 1995).

Clarifying which language to use, and in which contexts, should also involve determining the degree of competence students have in the language. For example, a child's conversational language proficiency may support contextually rich social interactions, but not the abstract discussions that typically accompany academic instruction based on written texts. Goals for such a student should prioritize further conversational language and concept development over formal instruction in reading, writing, or learning through print.

5. **Does instruction put the learning of literacy, including the text-based skills of reading and writing, in perspective with other educational goals for students using, for example, an Inquiry Model for Literacy across the curriculum (Bruce & Davidson, 1994)?**

The Inquiry Model for Literacy is based on a view similar to that described by Paul (1998) in his discussion of the literary critical perspective. According to Paul's discussion of this perspective, becoming literate is, above all, a matter of developing critical thinking skills. These thinking skills also apply to a variety of areas of knowledge, including technology (computer literacy), math, and others that enable one to contribute to and participate in society. In fact, according to this view, literacy is socially constructed by the participants in that society and determined according to cultural values. With this perspective, great literature may not even exist (p. 131); what is valued is determined by individuals in the context of their personal experience. Reading and writing, according to this view, are seen as one possible expression of thought. Furthermore, critical thinking is not dependent upon being able to read and write.

This perspective on literacy, held by many deaf people, implies an approach to children's education that is dramatically different from current approaches and should be considered. Presently, educational programs for deaf and hearing children are based on the view of development that children must learn to read and write before they can learn in other areas. The reason for this is that our society values print as the main way of obtaining information and furthering one's knowledge. Programs built on this view of learning heavily emphasize the teaching of reading and writing for a number of years. Indeed, it is the center of the curriculum.

However, putting learning to read and write at the center of the curriculum can lead to meaningless instruction for all students. It may harm deaf students (and many hearing students) in several additional ways:

▶ Developing competence in literacy in areas other than text-based skills may be overlooked (e.g., communicative competency, skills for social interaction, background knowledge, etc.). As a result, unmet needs in these areas may ultimately deter learning in reading and writing.

▶ Students may vary in their developmental readiness for this kind of instruction; some may need focus on continued development of skills from the previous level of development.

▶ By emphasizing learning to read and write, a long process and even longer when learned as a second language, learning other kinds of knowledge from non-print sources may be neglected.

An Inquiry Model for Literacy "assumes that knowledge is constructed through meaningful activity which may include, but is not limited to, conventional literacy activities" (Bruce & Davidson, 1994, p. 8). Reading and writing are still important in this model, but not in ways that exclude other modes of learning. In fact, Bruce and Davidson argue that, in this model, reading and writing become a more natural outgrowth of learning across the curriculum, rather than applied in artificial ways across curricular areas as they are in many "literacy across the curriculum" models. They explain that when literacy is applied to separately taught subject areas—or "across the curriculum"—these efforts often result in contrived reading and writing activities in these areas. In their model, inquiry—the exploration of ideas through discussion and social interaction— becomes the center of the curriculum. This approach is better suited to the broader view of literacy suggested in that it is more likely to develop other critical competencies *in addition* to text-based skills (e.g., language, critical thinking, conceptual knowledge about the world, and skills for collaboration and social interaction).

6. **Is a structured, balanced program of activities for teaching reading and writing implemented consistently throughout the program? Do the activities represent a balance between the ways that students learn—through acquisition and with instruction—and take into account individual differences?**

The previous guideline—putting reading and writing instruction into curricular perspective for deaf children—is not at odds with the suggestion to use a well-structured program to teach these skills. More concentrated efforts are needed to improve the *quality* of instruction in this area, including devoting more time to *authentic* reading and writing tasks, rather than the tedious paper-and-pencil activities that often fill instructional time.

One way to improve instruction is by implementing a well-structured, balanced framework of reading and writing activities across all levels of development. That framework should include establishing conditions for both ways in which children learn literacy: through acquisition and with instruction. The framework suggested here satisfies that criteria by representing a model of language and the learning of literacy based on the following conditions:

immersion, demonstration, expectation, responsibility, approximation, use and feedback (Cambourne, 1984). This model has been represented in curricular frameworks found in many sources (e.g., Cooper et al., 1997; Learning Media, Ministry of Education, 1985; Mooney, 1990; Routman, 1991; Strickland & Morrow, 1989). Typically, it includes the following activities:

- reading and writing aloud

- shared reading and writing

- guided reading and writing

- independent reading and writing

Each of these activities should occur daily, with the exception of guided reading and writing at the Emerging stage of development. However, the form these activities take—the balance between instruction and acquisition reflected in the activities—will vary for students at different levels of development. Examples of this variation are included in a more detailed description of these activities across developmental levels in **Appendix G**.

Activities will vary, too, according to instructional goals for individual students, even within the same level of development. The language used by the students is another variable influencing the shape of the activities. Activities for students learning written English as a second language should differ from those implemented for students learning to read and write English as their first language. Finally, the implementation of these activities should be a collaborative venture between home and school begun in early childhood, not the exclusive responsibility of the educational program. Given these considerations, each activity within the framework is summarized below:

Reading and Writing Aloud

During reading and writing aloud, students are *immersed* in language as read or written by another person. During these activities, written language is the vehicle for communicating ideas and stories; the language learning is incidental (acquired) and secondary to the content of the text. For that reason, reading aloud must involve language use that is comprehensible to the student, whether that language matches the text or not. If the language used differs from the text, as in the use of ASL, then successive rereading—once ideas are understood— may be used to more closely approximate the text language if this is a goal for some students (Erting & Pfau, 1997; Schleper, 1997). In a similar way, during writing aloud, students observe another person writing as that person explains what is being written (the message), using the child's conversational language.

During either of these activities, the student does not need to view the text and often does not. The focus is on what the reader or writer reads or explains about the text message. For example, young children, deaf or hearing, being read to at home most often look at the pictures accompanying stories—they are not typically expected to follow the print. The goals of reading aloud are to promote story enjoyment, to communicate information from texts that students may not access themselves, and to extend inquiry. Writing aloud has similar goals; both activities are used to *demonstrate* the uses of print as well.

Shared Reading and Writing

Shared reading and writing also can reformulate and extend ideas explored through inquiry, and these activities should arise from that context. During shared reading, the teacher reads to the students, extending invitations for students to participate as they wish. Proficient student readers may also lead this activity. During shared writing, the teacher or proficient student acts as scribe, and the group creates the text through conversation. During both of these activities, the written text is "shared"—viewed by all—allowing the reader or writer to demonstrate features of the written language. As with reading and writing aloud, the child's conversational language is used to discuss the text. These activities *demonstrate* reading and writing to students, helping them make associations between ideas, their conversational language, and written text. There is also an element of *expectation* in these activities as teachers invite students to join in if they wish—reading, or rereading, parts of text or contributing to the writing. This attitude of expectation—conveying the belief to students that they can learn to use written language—is an essential element in instruction.

Guided Reading and Writing

In these activities, students talk, think, and question their way through text as readers or writers with the teacher's support. Students *use* written language themselves to extend inquiry. During these activities, an increasing amount of *responsibility* is placed on the student for what he or she learns, both in kind and amount. Goal-setting with portfolios, for example, is one way to extend responsibility to students. As in the previous activities, adults' *expectations* about learning will influence the degree to which this happens. Too often children receive messages from adults that become self-limiting. ["How many ways can we give children the expectation that learning language-based skills is 'difficult,' 'complex,' 'beyond children'?" (Cambourne, 1984, p. 5).] Starting with students at the Beginning developmental stage of literacy, guided reading and writing become a critical part of their instruction in reading and writing, including mini-lessons targeted to their needs. During these activities, teachers must be aware of individual students' competencies, interests, and experiences in order to scaffold the experience successfully (Mooney, 1990). They must *demonstrate* new information in ways that will further learning and provide relevant *feedback* about students' use of language. In this context, teachers must create an instructional climate that is accepting of *approximations*—uses of language that do not display mature competence. Too often, especially with written work, students' approximations are critiqued as errors from an adult perspective, one that is based on competent use of language. Quantifying the errors in students' work (feedback through grades) is not as informative as providing constructive feedback—indicating strengths and providing information about selected, targeted errors. Furthermore, this practice—grading all errors—will undermine positive attitudes of expectancy.

Independent Reading and Writing

Independent reading and writing occur without the teacher's intervention or evaluation. The purpose of both is to build fluency and establish reading and writing as habits. As an outgrowth of inquiry, these activities encourage students to make personal connections, explore meanings, use critical thinking, and apply reading and writing in natural, pleasurable, self-chosen activities (Routman, 1991). A well-stocked, accessible library and a variety of tools for writing are musts. These activities promote the independent *use* of reading and writing, thus becoming another way that students take *responsibility* for their learning. They do not occur, however, unless teachers provide time and *expectation*.

In summary, the activities above represent a balanced framework for teaching reading and writing that applies across developmental levels. Implementation of these activities will vary not only according to level of development, but also according to individual strengths and needs, languages used, and language competence. Assessment should determine the nature of these variables in order to tailor activities to individual students. Finally, this framework does not exclude the use of other curricular materials; rather, it should structure their use.

7. **Are instructional goals for reading and writing selected according to *important skills and strategies* that individuals need—skills and strategies that actively engage students in both bottom-up and top-down processing of print?**

Teachers of all students, deaf or hearing, often feel pressured to cover—with even pacing—all of the material provided in an instructional program. As a result, many skills and objectives are taught with little but equal time invested in each. In other words, skills and objectives are not prioritized instructionally in ways that reflect their relative importance to learning to read and write. Furthermore, important skills are neglected when teaching reflects the "widespread assumption that skills and knowledge form a hierarchy or pyramid" (Anderson, 1994, p. 11). According to this pyramid, teaching starts at the base of a hierarchy with letter and word-level skills and considers mastery in these a prerequisite to learning the higher-level skills of "inquiry, problem solving, and reasoning" (p. 11). One outcome of this approach, according to research, is that high-ability reading groups spend more time in intellectually stimulating discussions than do low-ability reading groups (p.11). This finding for hearing children undoubtedly applies to the instruction of deaf children as well. Although educators may claim to emphasize critical thinking skills, such skills are often squeezed out of the curriculum for many students, deaf and hearing, when instruction focuses on low-level, bottom-up skills.

Students at all levels of development need instruction that will facilitate both top-down and bottom-up processing of print. With reference to the previous guideline, skills and strategies may be:

▶ acquired incidentally (e.g., through being read to, observing others writing, independent reading and writing),

▶ acquired through activities purposefully constructed to demonstrate their use (e.g., shared reading and writing), or

▶ learned through more direct instruction within the context of guided reading and writing activities.

One of the primary purposes of classroom assessment is to determine the nature of students' instructional needs—what skills and knowledge students are not acquiring and need to have demonstrated or taught directly in order to progress.

The following skills and strategies are important to the processes of reading, writing, or both. As a result, they represent areas of learning that have the potential to improve reading and writing through instruction—those that should be more explicitly demonstrated, or taught, to students according to need. These skills and strategies should be carefully monitored as students develop to determine that need. The reader is reminded, however, to approach assessment and instruction in the following ways with balanced consideration of the other interrelated guidelines for literacy planning.

Bottom-Up Processes of Reading and Writing:
Learning the Written Language

The purpose of these skills and strategies is to help students learn and apply knowledge of the cue systems used in English in order to read and write more accurately, automatically, and fluently. These systems are based on knowledge of the graphophonics, semantics, and syntax of English as discussed in Chapter 2. Hearing children typically acquire this knowledge through their acquisition of English as a spoken language. Subsequently, their first language's knowledge base helps these children understand how these same systems apply to reading and writing.

The challenge in teaching these skills to deaf children is to determine how they may be learned visually—what is the visual application or complement to these skills—and how they are best taught to learners who converse in a different language, such as ASL. Further, a teacher needs to recognize that instruction in these skills is increasingly difficult for students who lack a well-developed conversational language. This is another indication of the importance of early, conversational language acquisition to learning to read and write.

Word knowledge (vocabulary and decoding): Word knowledge and automatic recognition are highly associated with reading ability (e.g., Anderson, 1994; Paul, 1998). Students who read well (accurately and fluently) recognize many words in print without having to figure them out. Thus, an ongoing instructional goal should be to increase the bank of words in print that all children—deaf or hearing—recognize. One of the ways that older deaf students learn new vocabulary is by applying context clues (Davey & King, cited in Nickerson, 1996). For this reason, strategies to use these clues should be taught to younger students who need them. Also, students need to read widely in order to gain vocabulary in this way. In addition to incidental exposure to vocabulary through reading, students may be taught new words through the use of word banks, semantic maps, dictionary activities, and other meaningful vocabulary activities. These activities should be part of the exploration of ideas and information and never the result of exercises designed to teach words at random.

The Inquiry Model of Instruction in literacy previously suggested facilitates teaching vocabulary through the purposeful, contextual exploration of new concepts. In this model, the overlapping use of conversation, reading, and other means of obtaining information about a topic, such as videos, increases the likelihood that vocabulary will be committed to long-term memory as part of conceptual knowledge. The importance of learning vocabulary this way—as part of conceptual learning (as opposed to teaching random, individual words)—is reinforced by the finding that difficulty with vocabulary is related to conceptual difficulty (Anderson, 1994, p. 10). In other words, the harder it is to understand the concept behind a word, the harder it is to learn—and remember—the word itself. This is another reason why it makes sense to base vocabulary instruction on inquiry—questions that explore subjects in meaningful ways—and focus energy on teaching the related concepts in multiple ways, not just through print. Conceptual understanding may be a determining factor in the development of vocabulary.

Students also need skills for figuring out words they do not recognize automatically. Hearing children learn to do this with phonics (figuring out the individual sounds in written words), word analysis, and by using context clues. Deaf children frequently use context clues to figure out new words, as mentioned above; they may also decode new words visually using morphemic word analysis, learning to recognize the smaller meaning units within words—prefixes, suffixes, root words (Paul, 1998). For deaf students who can hear phonetic information—discriminate and identify the sounds in speech—decoding may also be taught phonetically, in much the same way that it is for hearing children. It should be taught separately from reading, however. Although the ability to discriminate segments of sound in words—phonetic awareness—is strongly associated with learning to read for hearing children, the extent to which deaf readers use this information, or how, needs further investigation.

Sentence level knowledge (syntax): Just as students need a bank of knowledge about words in print, they also need an internalized, accurate knowledge of English language structure. Irwin (1986) discusses teaching knowledge of sentence processing according to micro processes and integrative processes. The former refers to teaching students to recognize the ideas within sentences, the latter refers to teaching connections between and within sentences.

Irwin shows different ways to teach these skills. For example, she demonstrates how students can be taught to recognize idea units in sentences, assuming they know the individual words. Relying on sentence structure to help identify these ideas is part of the reading process and something that readers must learn to do automatically. Teachers can model how sentences are divided into phrases that organize words into ideas. The goal here is not to teach and have students practice identifying parts of sentences, but to show how language structure is used to further comprehension. Students need to be able to select and recall the important information in sentences as they read using knowledge of syntax as one cue.

Irwin explains, too, that as they read, readers must be able to connect ideas in sentences to a "coherent whole" (1986, p. 3) in order to remember the information. At the sentence level, she refers to this as the integrative process of reading. This process involves making connections between words and phrases used to denote the same ideas, e.g., Jack-he; sugary treats-candy; ran-dashed; …went *to the store* …went *there*. It also involves understanding when words denoting ideas are left out, but understood, such as, "I want some candy," followed by "I do, too." Further, readers must understand connectives used to relate ideas within sentences or between sentences, such as conjunctions (e.g., and, also), disjunctions (e.g., or, either/or), condition (e.g., if…then…), etc.

As mentioned, Irwin provides specific ideas about how to teach these processes and others in *Teaching Reading Comprehension Processes* (1986). She makes it clear, however, that this instruction is different from teaching language skills in isolation. It is teaching children how to do what good readers do—the processes they use to comprehend print. Although she is addressing the instructional needs of hearing children, many—if not most—deaf children need this instruction as well. It cannot be assumed that deaf children will acquire this knowledge incidentally, although some do. Knowledge and competence in the first language, whether it is ASL or a different spoken language, should be used to help students learn the structures of the English language through explanation and comparison to structures they know well through their conversational language.

Top-Down Processes of Reading: Comprehension Strategy Instruction

As previously stated, higher-level, top-down skills and strategies are often neglected as teachers aim for mastery of lower-level skills. In many cases, this delays the teaching of important top-down strategies to deaf students for years. Not only should these strategies be included in instruction for all levels of students, but the choice of strategies and the ways they are taught should also be given careful consideration. One promising area of research that lends itself to this goal is the study of *strategy instruction* (e.g., Garner, 1987; Palincsar and Brown, 1984; Pressley, Johnson et al., 1989). These studies have focused on teaching less proficient readers strategies they can use to help themselves understand and remember important ideas in texts. As with the language processes described in the previous section, the strategies themselves come from studies of those used automatically by proficient readers. These studies indicate that poorer readers either do not possess—or do not use—these strategies.

Proficient readers know many strategies or different ways to help them understand what they read, can describe how they use strategies, and are confident they can figure out what they read with these strategies. For example, they are competent at deciphering the main ideas in what they read. On the surface, some of these strategies may seem to be similar to the skills found in traditional activities for reading comprehension. However, Kelly (1992) points out that there is an important difference between the two, similar to Irwin's (1986) distinction between language process instruction and traditional skills instruction. Traditional comprehension activities focus on having students apply a skill, such as determining the main idea, to a given text with that task being the end goal of instruction. Strategy instruction focuses on teaching students a set of behaviors (strategies often involve a number of steps) that they can use to help them understand new texts. The end goal is learning to apply the strategy so that it facilitates comprehension with different texts. Thus, strategy instruction involves teaching:

- how to summarize text by selecting the main ideas (i.e., the behaviors associated with the strategy,

- how to self-activate the use of strategies, and

- how to determine appropriate use of strategies (knowing which strategy to use when).

Strategy instruction is greatly oversimplified in this discussion. In reality, this instruction must be approached with thoughtful planning in order for it to succeed. First of all, strategies should be carefully chosen. Research indicates that a select number of strategies have proven to make a difference in reading achievement (e.g., Garner, 1987; Pressley, Johnson et al., 1989). Some of these are listed below. Second, research also indicates that strategies are best learned through direct instruction that includes reflective use, feedback, and extensive application (e.g., Garner, 1987; Pressley, Johnson et al., 1989; Paris et al., 1991). Instruction is an ongoing process. The procedures for teaching strategies have been carefully defined in the literature. Finally, the success of strategy instruction appears to rely on students' beliefs about their abilities to further their comprehension (e.g., Pressley, Goodchild et al., 1989). Attending to these beliefs is an important part of the instructional process. For further information about strategy instruction, readers are advised to consult the growing amount of published work in this area, including the references given above.

Some of the strategies best known for improving reading comprehension include:

Story Structure (e.g., Pressley, Johnson et al., 1989): Students who have an internalized sense of story, either from someone's reading or telling them stories or from reading themselves, are more likely to understand and remember new stories. Students can be taught story structure and how to use this information as well. The goal of this strategy is to help students apply knowledge of story structure to understand and remember new stories.

Making Inferences—Activation of Prior Knowledge (e.g., Dole, Duffy, Roehler, & Pearson, 1991; Garner, 1987; Pressley, Johnson et al., 1989): Students who can use their background knowledge to figure out relationships in texts are better able to understand what they are reading. These relationships may be explicitly stated in the text, or they may be implied. Deaf students can, and should, learn to more effectively apply what they know to help them comprehend written text.

Summarization (e.g., Dole et al., 1991; Garner, 1987; Pressley, Johnson et al., 1989): The ability to summarize the main ideas in a text is an indication of comprehension and enables readers to remember important information. Although summarization is a complex skill, there are specific steps that mature readers can learn to apply to this strategy. Also, the rudiments of summarization can be learned by students at all levels if they are taught to consider what a passage or story is "about."

Mental imagery (e.g., Tierney & Pearson, as cited in Tierney & Cunningham, 1984; Pressley, Johnson et al., 1989): Using mental imagery to further comprehension has succeeded with some readers. This strategy involves having children—those who can process concrete, written text—form mental pictures of scenarios they read. This strategy can be easily taught; it also seems to facilitate remembering important information as well as understanding it.

Monitoring Comprehension (e.g., Garner, 1987; Paris et al., 1991): Good readers monitor their comprehension, checking themselves when they do not understand what they are reading. When this happens, they use strategies such as looking back, reading ahead to see if confusion is resolved, or using other information (headings, pictures, etc.) to clarify meaning. Awareness of one's comprehension and steps to fix comprehension breakdowns can be taught.

These strategies, and others, should be sources of instruction for deaf children (Kelly, 1992). Both the selection and approach to strategy instruction should be determined by the developmental level of the student. For example, most strategies, as they are discussed in the literature, are taught to students who are Developing or Maturing readers. However, exposure to strategies can and should be provided at earlier stages of development as concepts unrelated to print. For example, Emerging readers can discuss the parts of a story that have been told to them by answering such questions as, "Who were the main characters? What did they do? How did the story end?" Strategy instruction with deaf children should be influenced by language use as well. In other words, strategies should be discussed in ASL and used with conversational "texts" in this language and in other non-print ways before they are applied to reading. As suggested in the literature, a few strategies should be selected for instruction and taught thoroughly.

Writing Process Skills and Strategies

Assumptions about the pyramid approach to learning—that lower-level skills must be learned before higher-level skills—are evident in the instruction of writing for deaf children just as they are in approaches designed to teach reading. Teaching often focuses on the sentence level skills and conventions of writing; lack of mastery in these prevents many students from receiving instruction in higher-level thinking and reasoning skill. This is despite the finding that higher level skills make the difference between good and poor deaf writers (Gormley & Sarachan-Daily, cited in Paul, 1998). In this study, two groups of deaf writers—distinguished by level of proficiency—made the same amount and kind of linguistic and surface errors. However, the better writers tended to have more cohesive, developed texts. They seemed to have a better sense of audience.

This finding, reinforced by the previous discussion about including both top-down and bottom-up skills in instruction, implies a need for using a process approach to teaching writing. In this way, both top-down and bottom-up processes can be sorted out instructionally. It also implies the need to emphasize audience awareness by using writing for authentic communication. The more students are exposed to readers' natural responses to their writing—not critical judgments—the quicker they learn to focus on clarifying meaning.

As part of instruction, teachers should show students how to use strategies that could improve their writing. As described in Chapter 2, good writers are more reflective, put more time into planning, and reread their writing more often as they write (Krashen, 1992). They also tend to focus on meaning, rather than mechanics, when they revise. As with reading comprehension strategies, these behaviors can be taught to students.

With a process approach, students can separate the tasks involved in writing in order to develop thinking skills in addition to sentence-level and mechanical skills. Planning what to write need not involve paper and pencil. In fact, planning for writing should proceed with extensive thinking and development of ideas through conversation before students begin to write. Drafting should be free of concern for errors, and editing should allow students to focus on mechanical issues without having to work on meaning at the same time.

Many teachers who use a process approach with students who converse in ASL advise having these students develop concepts in ASL before attempting to express them in writing. Mahshie (1995), for example, discusses how some teachers use "process signing" (p. 50) to have students plan as well as present "texts" in signed language (citing Foss Ahlden & Lundin, 1994). In this way, students learn to fully create and communicate different genre—usually represented in writing—in their first language before attempting the same in a written second language. The process usually associated with instruction in writing—planning, drafting, revision, and presentation—is followed in the development of the signed text. Finally, translating into written text (working with the teacher, in small groups or independently depending on the level of readiness) allows students not only to create a polished English text, but also to make connections between the structures of their two languages in the process.

Conclusion

In summary, the seven guidelines suggested above describe conditions for instruction in literacy and planning that deaf children need in order to progress. These guidelines represent the following concepts:

1. a broad view of literacy,

2. instruction and assessment that are guided by development,

3. language use that is fully accessible and comprehensible,

4. language role clarification,

5. a model of inquiry for literacy across the curriculum,

6. a balanced framework of activities for teaching reading and writing, and

7. the selection of important top-down and bottom-up skills and strategies or teaching reading and writing.

Along with these guidelines, there are two factors that should be stressed. One of these is the role of instruction in literacy within the broader goals of education, a subject discussed in several places throughout this text.

As mentioned, instruction in literacy should not overshadow or be separate from what children learn of other kinds of knowledge. Literacy involves the communication of thoughts and the process of learning *through* conversation, reading, and writing. To teach any of these three as the end goals of instruction—devoid of concepts and critical thinking—is to defeat the purpose of learning these skills and will most likely result in failed instruction. However, such practices are common in instructional programs for elementary students, deaf and hearing. They are practices that a) do not motivate students and b) hinder students' potential to further their learning.

The other factor that influences the outcome of instruction concerns the social climate of the classroom. Writing about hearing children, Anderson (1994) explains that "the individual is the creature of culture, and thus, learning and development must be construed as socially situated" (p. 3). Tierney and Cunningham (1984) raise the same issue when they make a plea for researchers of reading to have a "vision of learning groups" (p. 640), to guide research efforts. They elaborate by saying that learning is a social event and that the nature of the learning community cannot be disregarded in research or in practice. The characteristics of the group influence learning as much as those of the individual learners themselves.

Fischgrund (1996) makes a similar point with reference to deaf children: "language acquisition, literacy, and learning and all of the skills associated with these processes depend upon human interaction, facilitation, and encouragement" (p. 2). Literacy, regardless of how it is approached instructionally, will not develop in a vacuum. This, too, is a way that instructional programs often fail deaf students. Two conditions must prevail in order for these students to benefit from the social dynamics of learning: 1) interaction and collaborative learning must be an accepted part of instruction, and 2) the conversational language of the classroom must be fully accessible to all.

Finally, when planning for literacy instruction, the most important message of this chapter is that methodology should be driven by individual need. Too often in literacy programs for deaf children, this point is overlooked in the sincere attempt to make a difference.

References

Anderson, R. C. & Pearson, P. D. (1984). A schema-theoretic view of basic processes in reading comprehension. In P. D. Pearson, R. Barr, M. L. Kamil, & P. Mosenthal (Eds.), *Handbook of Reading Research* (pp. 255-293). New York: Longman.

Anderson, R. C. (1994). *The Future of Reading Research* (Tech. Rep. No. 600). Champaign: University of Illinois at Urbana-Champaign, College of Education, Center for the Study of Reading.

Anthony, R. J., Johnson, T. D., Mickelson, N. I., & Preece, A. (1991). *Evaluating Literacy: A Perspective for Change*. Portsmouth, NH: Heinemann.

Bachman, L. F. (1990). *Fundamental Considerations in Language Testing*. UK: Oxford University Press.

Baker, L. & Brown, A. L. (1984). Metacognitive skills and reading. In P. D. Pearson (Ed.), *Handbook of Reading Research* (pp. 353-395). New York: Longman.

Barrs, M., Ellis, S., Hester, H., & Thomas, A. (1989). *The Primary Language Record: A Handbook for Teachers*. Portsmouth, NH: Heinemann.

Brown, A. L. (1980). Metacognitive development and reading. In R. J. Spiro, B. C. Bruce, & W. F. Brewer (Eds.), *Theoretical Issues in Reading Comprehension*. Hillsdale, NJ: Erlbaum.

Brualdi, C. B. (1986). *Multiple Intelligences: Gardner's Theory*. Washington, DC: ERIC Clearinghouse on Assessment and Evaluation, The Catholic University of America. (Eric/AE Digest Series EDO-TM-96-01).

Bruce, B. C. & Davidson, B. D. (1994). *An Inquiry Model for Literacy Across the Curriculum* (Tech. Rep. No. 598). Champaign: University of Illinois at Urbana-Champaign, College of Education, Center for the Study of Reading.

Bruner, J. S. (1975). The ontogenesis of speech acts. *The Journal of Child Language, 2,* 1-40.

Calfee, R. & Hiebert, E. (1991). Classroom assessment in reading. In R. Barr, M. L. Kamil, P. Mosenthal, & P. D. Pearson (Eds.), *Handbook of Reading Research: Volume II* (pp. 281-309). New York: Longman.

Cambourne, B. (1984). *Language, Learning, and Literacy* (reproduced from *Towards a Reading-Writing Classroom* by permission of Primary English Teaching Association, Sydney, Australia). Crystal Lake, IL: Rigby.

Carroll, D. & Carini, P. (1991). Tapping teachers' knowledge. In V. Perrone (Ed.), *Expanding Student Assessment* (pp. 40-46). Alexandria, VA: Association for Supervision and Curriculum Development.

Chall, J. S. (1983). *Stages of Reading Development*. New York: McGraw-Hill.

Chittenden, E. (1991). Authentic assessment, evaluation, and documentation of student performance. In V. Perrone (Ed.), *Expanding Student Assessment* (pp. 22-31). Alexandria, VA: Association for Supervision and Curriculum Development.

Clay, M. M. (1972). *The Early Detection of Reading Difficulties: A Diagnostic Survey with Recovery Procedures*. Auckland: Heinemann Educational Books (3rd ed., 1985).

Cooper, W., Barr, M., & McKittrick, A. (Eds.). (1995). *The Primary Language Record & the California Learning Record in Use*. El Cajon, CA: The Center for Language in Learning.

Cooper, J. D., Pilulski, J. J., Au, K., Carlderon, M., Comas, J. C., Lipson, M. Y., Mims, J. S., Page, S. E., Valencia, S. W., & Vogt, M. (1997). *Professional Development Handbook: Invitations to Literacy*. Boston: Houghton Mifflin.

Davies, S. [currently Mahshie] (1994). Attributes for success: Attitudes and practices that facilitate the transition to bilingualism in Sweden and Denmark. In I. Ahlgren & K. Hyltenstam (Eds.), *Bilingualism in Deaf Education: Proceedings of the International Conference on Bilingualism in Deaf Education, Stockholm, Sweden*. International Studies on Sign Language and Communication of the Deaf, Vol. 27. Hamburg, Germany: Signum Press.

Dole, J. A., Duffy, G. G., Roehler, L. R., Pearson, P. D. (1991). Moving from the old to the new: Research on reading comprehension instruction. *Review of Educational Research, 61 (2)*, 239-264.

Duran, R. P. (1988). Validity and language skills assessment: Non-English background students. In H. Wainer & H. I. Braun (Eds.), *Test Validity*. Hillsdale, NJ: Lawrence Erlbaum Associates.

Erting, L. & Phau, J. (1997). *Becoming Bilingual: Facilitating English Literacy Development Using ASL in PreSchool* (Occasional paper). Washington, DC: Gallaudet University Pre-College National Mission Programs.

Ewoldt, C. (1981). A psycholinguistic description of selected deaf children. *Reading Research Quarterly, 1,* 58-89.

Fishgrund, J. E. (1991, November). *Language and Communication Issues: Where Have We Been—Where are We Now?* Paper presented at the 10th Annual Language Coordinators Workshop at the Pennsylvania School for the Deaf, Philadelphia, PA.

Foss Ahlden, H., & Lundin, K. (1994). *Language workshop in grade 3: A process-oriented working method in a bilingual school for the deaf.* Orebro, Sweden: SIH Laromedel.

Flynt, E. S. & Cooter, R. B. (1995). *Reading Inventory for the Classroom.* Scottsdale, AZ: Gorsuch Scarisbrick, Publishers.

French, M. M., Hallau, M. G., & Ewoldt, C. (1985). *Kendall Demonstration Elementary School Language Arts Curriculum Guide* (second edition, no longer in print). Washington, DC: Pre-College Programs, Gallaudet University.

Francis, J. M., Garner, D. H., & Harvey, J. H. T. (1980). *KDES Language Curriculum Guide: A Pragmatic Approach to Language for Teachers of Deaf Children* (no longer in print). Washington, DC: Kendall Demonstration Elementary School, Gallaudet University.

Gardner, H. (1983). *Frames of Mind.* New York: Basic Book, Inc.

Garner, R. (1987). *Metacognition and Reading Comprehension.* Norwood, NJ: Ablix Publishing Corporation.

Glazer, S. & Brown, C. (1993). *Portfolios and Beyond: Collaborative Assessment in Reading and Writing.* Norwood, MA: Christopher-Gordon Publishers, Inc.

Gleason, J. B. (1993). Language development: An overview and a preview. In J. B. Gleason (Ed.), *The Development of Language.* New York: Macmillan Publishing Company.

Goodman, Y. M. & Burke, Y. M. (1980). *Reading Strategies: Focus on Comprehension.* New York: Holt, Rinehard and Winston.

Goodman, K. (1986). *What's Whole in Whole Language?* Portsmouth, NH: Heinemann.

Goodman, Y. (1989). Evaluation of students: Teachers of evaluation. In Goodman, K. S.,

Goodman, Y. M. & Hood, W. J. (Eds.), *The Whole Language Evaluation Book.* Portsmouth, NH: Heinemann.

Goodman, K. S. (1976). The Goodman taxonomy of reading miscues. In P. D. Allen & D. Watson (Eds.), *Findings of Research in Miscue Analysis: Classroom Applications*. Urbana, IL: National Council of Teachers of English.

Goodman, K. (1986). *What's Whole in Whole Language?* Portsmouth, NH: Heinemann.

Graney, S. (1997). *Where Does Speech Fit In? Spoken English in a Bilingual Context*. Washington, DC: Gallaudet University Pre-College National Mission Programs.

Graves, D. H. (1991). *Build a Literate Classroom*. Portsmouth, NH: Heinemann.

Hanson, L. L. & Mosqueira, J. (1995). *ASL to English Strategies: A Bilingual Approach*. Paper presented at a meeting of the Teachers of English to Speakers of Other Languages (TESOL), Long Beach, CA.

Hartman, J. A. & Hartman, D. K. (1994). *Arranging Multi-text Reading Experiences that Expand the Reader's Role* (Tech. Rep. No. 604). Champaign: University of Illinois at Urbana-Champaign, College of Education, Center for the Study of Reading.

Herman, J. L., Aschbacher, P. R., & Winters, L. (1992). *A Practical Guide to Alternative Assessment*. Alexandria, VA: Association for Supervision and Curriculum Development.

Hoskisson, K. & Tompkins, G. E. (1987). *Language Arts: Content and Teaching Strategies*. Columbus, Ohio: Merrill Publishing Company.

Irwin, J. W. (1986). *Teaching Reading Comprehension Processes*. Englewood Cliffs, NJ: Prentice Hall, Inc.

Israelite, J., Ewoldt, C., & Hoffmeister, R. (1989). *A Review of the Literature on the Effective Use of Native Sign Language on the Acquisition of a Majority Language by Hearing Impaired Students*. Toronto, Canada: MGS Publication Services.

Johnson, T., Anthony, R., Field, J., Mickelson, N., & Preece, A. (1988). *Evaluation: A Perspective for Change*. Crystal City, IL: Rigby.

Johnson, R. E., Liddell, S. K., & Erting, C. J. (1989). *Unlocking the Curriculum: Principles for Achieving Access in Deaf Education* (Gallaudet Research Institute Working Paper 89-3). Washington, DC: Gallaudet University.

Johnston, P. & Allington, R. (1991). Remediation. In R. Barr, M. L. Kamil, P. B. Mosenthal, & P. D. Pearson (Eds.), *Handbook of Reading Research: Volume II* (pp. 984-1012). New York: Longman.

Johnston, P. H. (1984). Assessment in reading. In P. D. Pearson (Ed.), *Handbook of Reading Research* (pp. 147-182). New York: Longman.

Kelly, L. (1992). *The Cognitive View of Reading Processes.* Unpublished manuscript, Gallaudet University, Washington, DC.

Krashen, S. D. (1992). *Fundamentals of Language Education*. Torrance, CA: Laredo Publishing Co.

Krashen, S. D. (1984). *Writing: Research, Theory and Applications*. Torrance, CA: Laredo Publishing Co.

Lane, H. (1992). Educating the American Sign Language-speaking minority of the United States: A paper prepared for the Commission on the Education of the Deaf. In S. Wilcox, (Ed.), *Academic Acceptance of American Sign Language* (Sign Language Studies Monograph). Burtonsville, MD: Linstok Press.

Learning Media: Ministry of Education. (1985). *Reading in Junior Classes*. Wellington, New Zealand: author. Distributed by R. C. Owen, Inc., NY.

Leslie, L. (1993). A developmental-interactive approach to reading instruction. *Reading & Writing Quarterly: Overcoming Learning Difficulties, 9* (1), 5-30.

Mahshie, S. N. (1995). *Educating Deaf Children Bilingually*. Washington, DC: Gallaudet University Pre-College Programs.

Mahshie, S. N. (1997). *A First Language: Whose Choice Is It?* Washington, DC: Gallaudet University Pre-College National Mission Programs.

McTighe, J. & Ferrara, S. (1994). *Assessing Learning in the Classroom* (Rep. from Professional Standards and Practice). Washington, DC: National Educational Association.

Meier, R. P. (1991). Language acquisition by deaf children. *American Scientist, 79*, 60-70.

Miller, W. H. (1995). *Alternative Assessment Techniques for Reading and Writing*. New York: The Center for Applied Research in Education.

Mooney, M. E. (1990). *Reading To, With, And By Children*. Katonah, NY: Richard C. Owen Publishers, Inc.

Newport, E. L. & Meier, R. P. (1985). The acquisition of American Sign Language. In D. I. Slobin (Ed.), *The Cross-linguistic Study of Language Acquisition, Vol. I* (pp. 881-937). Hillsdale, NJ: Lawrence Erlbaum Associates.

References

Nickerson, J. F. (1996). *Using Literacy Portfolios to Promote Deaf Students' Engagement in Self-assessment*. Unpublished doctoral dissertation, University of Maryland, College Park.

Nover, S. M. & Andrews, J. (1998). *Critical Pedagogy in Deaf Education: Bilingual Methodology and Staff Development*. USCLC Star Schools Project Report No. 1. Santa Fe, NM: New Mexico School for the Deaf.

O'Donnell, M. P. & Wood, M. (1992). *Becoming a Reader: A Developmental Approach to Reading Instruction*. Boston: Allyn and Bacon.

Palincsar, A. S. & Brown, A. L. (1984). Reciprocal teaching of comprehension-fostering and comprehension-monitoring activities. *Cognition and Instruction*, 1 (2), 117-175.

Paris, S. G., Wasick, B. A., & Turner, J. C. (1991). The development of strategic readers. In R. Barr, M. L. Kamil, P. B. Mosenthal, & P. D. Pearson (Eds.), *Handbook of Reading Research: Volume II* (pp. 609-640). New York: Longman.

Paul, P. V. (1998). *Literacy and Deafness: The Development of Reading, Writing, and Literate Thought*. Needham Heights, MA: Allyn & Bacon.

Pearson, P. D. & Fielding, L. (1991). Comprehension instruction. In R. Barr, M. L. Kamil, P. B. Mosenthal, & P. D. Pearson (Eds.), *Handbook of Reading Research: Volume II* (pp. 815-860). New York: Longman.

Pettito, L. A. (1993). *On the Linguistic Status of Natural Signed Languages*. Unpublished manuscript, McGill University Department of Psychology.

Peyton, J., French, M. et al. (1993). *Teaming with Text: Computer Networks to Develop Deaf Students' Written English*. Washington, DC: Gallaudet University. (ERIC Document Reproduction Service No. 357 616)

Peyton, J. & French, M. (1996). *Making English Accessible: Using Electronic Networks for Interaction in the Classroom*. Washington, DC: Gallaudet University Pre-College National Mission Programs.

Pierce, L. V. & O'Malley, J. M. (1992). *Performance and Portfolio Assessment for Language Minority Students* (Program Information Guide Series, Report No. 9). Washington, DC: National Clearinghouse for Bilingual Education.

Pinker, S. (1994). *The Language Instinct*. New York: Harper Perennial.

Popham, W. J. (1995). *Classroom Assessment: What Teachers Need to Know*. Boston: Allyn and Bacon.

Pressely, M., Goodchild, F., Fleet, J., & Zajchowski, E. (1989). The challenges of classroom strategy instruction. *The Elementary School Journal, 89 (3)* 301-342.

Pressley, M., Johnson, C. J., Symons, S., McGoldrick, J. A., & Kurita, J. A. (1989). Strategies that improve children's memory and comprehension of text. *The Elementary School Journal, 90 (1)*, 3-32.

Rhodes, L. K. & Shankin, N. (1993). *Windows into Literacy: Assessing Learners K-8.* Portsmouth, NH: Heinemann.

Routman, R. (1991). *Invitations: Changing as Teachers and Learners K-12.* Portsmouth, NH: Heinemann.

Samuels, S. J. & Kamil, M. L. (1984). Models of the reading process. In P. D. Pearson (Ed.), *Handbook of Reading Research* (pp. 185-224). New York: Longman.

Schleper, D. R. (1992). *Prereading Strategies.* Washington, DC: Gallaudet University Pre-College National Mission Programs.

Schleper, D. R. (1997). *Reading to Deaf Children: Learning from Deaf Adults.* Washington, DC: Pre-College National Mission Programs, Gallaudet University.

Schleper, D. R. (1998). *Read It Again and Again.* Washington, DC: Pre-College National Mission Programs, Gallaudet University.

Stanovich, K. E. (1980). Toward an interactive-compensatory model of individual differences in the development of reading fluency. *Reading Research Quarterly, 1,* 32-71.

Strickland, D. & Morrow, L. (1989). *Emerging Literacy: Young Children Learn to Read and Write.* Newark, DE: International Reading Association.

Sweet, A. P. (1993). *State of the Art: Transforming Ideas for Teaching and Learning to Read* (GPO Stock No. 065-000-00620-1). Washington, DC: U.S. Department of Education, Office of Educational Research and Improvement.

Syverson, P. (1995). Integration of the learning record in computer-enhanced classrooms. In W. Cooper & M. Barr (Eds.), *The Primary Language Record & the California Learning Record in Use* (pp. 26-28). El Cajon, CA: The Center for Language in Learning.

Tierney, R. J. & Cunningham, J. W. (1984). Research on teaching reading comprehension. In P. D. Pearson (Ed.), *Handbook of Reading Research* (pp. 609-656). New York: Longman.

Tierney, J., Carter, M. A., & Desai, L. E. (1991). *Portfolio Assessment in the Reading-Writing Classroom.* Norwood, MA: Christopher-Gordon Publishers, Inc.

Vygotsky, L. S. (1978). *Mind in Society*. Cambridge, MA: Harvard University Press.

Weaver, C. (1988). *Reading Process and Practice*. Portsmouth, NH: Heinemann Educational Books

Welsh-Charrier, C. C. (1991). *The Literature Journal*. Washington, DC: Gallaudet University Pre-College National Mission Programs.

Wittrock, M. C. (1979). The cognitive movement in instruction. *Educational Researcher, 8,* 5-11.

Woodward, J. (1978). Some sociolinguistic problems in the implementation of bilingual education for deaf students. In W. Stokoe (Ed.), *Proceedings of the National Symposium on Sign Language Research and Teaching*. Silver Spring, MD: National Association of the Deaf.

Zemelman, S., Daniels, H., & Hyde, A. (1993). *Best practice: New standards for Teaching and Learning in America's Schools*. Portsmouth, NH: Heinemann.

Index